SEAT OF EMPIRE

ROBERTA J. M. OLSON *AND* MARGARET K. HOFER

WITH AN ESSAY BY BERNARD CHEVALLIER

THE NEW-YORK HISTORICAL SOCIETY

PUBLISHED BY

The New-York Historical Society
Two West 77th Street
New York, New York 10024
www.nyhistory.org

This catalogue was produced in conjunction with the
exhibition *Seat of Empire*, held at the New-York Historical
Society from October 8, 2002 to January 12, 2003.

MANAGING EDITOR: Nancy Eklund Later
DESIGNER: Sara E. Stemen

This project is generously supported by the New York State
Council on the Arts, a State Agency.

AmericanAirlines
New York's Bridge to the World.

American Airlines, the official airline
of the New-York Historical Society

CONTENTS

PREFACE

THE NOVEMBER 2000 opening of the Henry Luce III Center for the Study of American Culture at the New-York Historical Society represented an investment in the interpretive potential of the institution's remarkable collection of decorative arts and material culture. Although the Society's formidable holdings of American portraits, Hudson River School masterworks, Tiffany lamps, and Audubon watercolors were known to scholars and art enthusiasts, only the most determined of researchers had investigated the depth of historical artifacts accrued by the Society's Museum.

Deterring the modern study of this material was its limited access in off-site storage. Removed from convenient sight, the collection indeed fulfilled the prediction that it would fall out of the minds of those reshaping the field of material culture. The Luce Center's debut enabled the Society to gain unprecedented intellectual and physical control of its fine arts and material culture holdings.

Seat of Empire exemplifies our recent efforts to explore intriguing speculations long associated with a range of diverse artifacts and "relics." Launched with the presentation of *Fit for a King* in 2000, this series of "block-chipper" exhibitions was conceived as a platform for exploring the complex cultural history encoded in singular objects—to date, reconstructing the lineage of two rare French-made chairs—and for showing how different investigative approaches can join forces to yield meanings larger than the sum of an artifact's parts. Both of these case studies—and those planned for future presentation—attempt to illuminate the universe of contemporary ideas, events, ownership habits, symbolic functions, and design ambitions present at the object's time of creation.

To the scrupulous research of New-York Historical Society curators Margaret K. Hofer and Roberta J. M. Olson over the past sixteen months we owe the rehabilitated provenance of the grand *fauteuil* central to this exhibition. By authenticating the armchair's storied origins and former function in Napoleon's council chamber at Malmaison, they have also restored a prime document for the ongoing study of culture's transatlantic flow between the young United States and Napoleonic France. Assisting them has been a network of colleagues here and abroad, whose expertise helped determine the strategies for conserving the chair and confirming its migration from Napoleon's château west of Paris to the Empire city of New York, with a lay-over in the Bordentown, New Jersey estate of Joseph Bonaparte, the First Consul's taste-conscious elder brother. What emerges in *Seat of Empire* is the historical context for the chair's 1867 rite-of-passage into the trove of pedigreed "eye-witness" objects then being gathered by the New-York Historical Society. Thanks to the thorough work of all who contributed to the project, it is also possible to freshly appreciate why a consular seat commissioned by a power-intoxicated French emperor deserves its diplomatic place in the New-York Historical Society's Luce Center, which claims the "study of American culture" as its mission. We are grateful to our funders for their generous support of *Seat of Empire*, and to our lenders for allowing the Society to assemble a persuasive material and visual argument on behalf of the chair's pre-Manhattan, pre-museum past.

Jan Seidler Ramirez
VICE PRESIDENT AND MUSEUM DIRECTOR
THE NEW-YORK HISTORICAL SOCIETY

ACKNOWLEDGMENTS

Seat of Empire, the exhibition it accompanies, and the conservation of the Napoleon armchair were made possible with the generous support of the Samuel H. Kress Foundation. Additional support was provided by the Florence Gould Foundation and the Dillon Fund. All programs of the New-York Historical Society are made possible with support from the New York City Department of Cultural Affairs and the New York State Council on the Arts, a State Agency. Travel was sponsored by American Airlines.

We are greatly indebted to many colleagues in the United States and Europe, especially in France, for graciously facilitating our quest for information about Napoleon's *fauteuil*. Special thanks go to the staff of the New-York Historical Society, as well as to Alexandra Mazzitelli and Valerie Paley for their invaluable contributions to the project. Above all, we owe deep gratitude to Bernard Chevallier, Director and Chief Curator of Malmaison, for serving as consultant to the exhibition and for sharing with us, both at Malmaison and via a flurry of transatlantic correspondence, his profound knowledge of this historic site and its rich collections.

Roberta J. M. Olson
ASSOCIATE CURATOR OF DRAWINGS
THE NEW-YORK HISTORICAL SOCIETY

Margaret K. Hofer
ASSOCIATE CURATOR OF DECORATIVE ARTS
THE NEW-YORK HISTORICAL SOCIETY

FIGURE 1

Jacob Frères, Armchair (*fauteuil*) from the Salle du Conseil at Malmaison, 1800 (CHECKLIST NO. 1)

FIGURE 2

Virtual restoration of armchair in Figure 1

FIGURES 3 AND 4

Pierre-Joseph Petit, *View of the Garden Facade of the Château of Malmaison*, ca. 1802–07, Musée national du château de Malmaison (MM.40.47.591)

Jean-Victor Nicolle, *View of the Cour d'honneur of the Château of Malmaison*, ca. 1810 (CHECKLIST NO. 13)

THE SETTING:

MALMAISON AND THE SALLE DU CONSEIL

BERNARD CHEVALLIER

DIRECTOR AND CHIEF CURATOR OF MALMAISON

IMAGINE OUR EXCITEMENT at Malmaison in learning of the armchair from the château's council room in the collection of the New-York Historical Society (FIGURE 1), believed to have belonged to Napoleon's brother Joseph Bonaparte. Having survived largely intact, it retains its original gilding, painted wood surface, and the original upholstery embellished with black velvet and gold trim.

When Josephine, wife of Napoleon Bonaparte, purchased Malmaison on 21 April 1799, the apartment belonging to the mistress of the house (Madame Le Couteulx du Molay) occupied the north side of the ground floor of the château (FIGURES 3 AND 4).[1] During the Consulate, this fourteenth-century château—rebuilt in the 1600s on the site occupied since the ninth century—served as Napoleon and Josephine's primary residence. In 1800 Napoleon decided to transform one of the rooms in the ground-floor apartment, initially used as his sleeping chamber, into a council room (salle du conseil) to accommodate his frequent cabinet meetings. The architect responsible for the job, Pierre-François-Léonard Fontaine, along with his friend and partner Charles Percier, recalled: "The First Consul had ordered a council room. The layout and decoration had to be completed in ten days, because he did not want his frequent visits interrupted; as a result, it seemed fitting to design the room in the form of a tent supported by pikestaffs, war tro-

phies, and insignia, interspersed with suspended trophies recalling history's most celebrated soldiers."[2] Aside from the striped fabric with red and yellow fringe draping the walls and ceiling, the room's only ornament consisted of a series of eight trophies (paired swords and helmets) painted on the two sets of double doors opening into the dining room and the library (FIGURE 5). Painted after the designs of Percier, they represented Carthaginian, Roman, Greek, chivalric, Gallic, Dacian, Persian, and Etruscan armor. Although these paintings survive largely intact, the pikestaffs and trophies were repainted during the restorations of 1900, and the tented fabric was restored to its original form in 1972.

The furniture, commissioned in 1800 from Jacob Frères, is known from the inventory taken after the death of Josephine (1814), who left the room untouched after the couple's divorce in 1809. Uniformly covered in red upholstery outlined with a black velvet and gold trim, the room's furnishings consisted of no less than twenty-eight seats: two sofas (lits de repos) on either side of the fireplace, each decorated with two pillows; ten large armchairs (fauteuils); ten stools (tabourets), all made of wood painted to resemble bronze and gilded; together with six mahogany chairs (chaises).[3] This suite of furniture remained in the room after the 1824 death of Prince Eugène, son of Josephine,[4] but was sold in the large sale of

FIGURE 5

Charles Percier and Pierre-François-Léonard Fontaine, the Salle du Conseil at Malmaison,
plate 55 in the *Recueil de décorations intérieures comprenant tout ce qui a rapport à l'ameublement*, 1801 (CHECKLIST NO. 28)

Malmaison furniture carried out at the château between 27 May and 31 July 1829.[5] While six chairs were auctioned as a group to Monsieur Fabien for 107 francs, the stools were sold in pairs to different bidders at prices ranging from 36 to 94 francs for both! Nine of the ten armchairs also came under the gavel, each one fetching between 70 and 100 francs. The tenth, reportedly used by the emperor and marked by him on its armrests with a penknife, was retained by the family and in 1851 was part of the collection of the Duke of Leuchtenberg, son of Prince Eugène.[6] The remaining two *lits de repos* found buyers for 212 and 200 francs, respectively. Among the chief purchasers was General Gourgaud, companion to the emperor on

St. Helena, who acquired the two *lits de repos*, two stools, and two armchairs for himself. Soon thereafter, in 1835 he sold all but the armchairs for unknown reasons.[7]

Today three of the original stools (FIGURE 12) are in Malmaison's Salle du Conseil. In 1990 they were joined by two stools of the same model made for the ceremonial bedroom of the Elysée palace in 1806, which belonged to Joachim Murat—Napoleon's brother-in-law, the first Grand Duke of Berg, and later King of Naples (1808).[8] Although the mahogany console placed between the windows has not been recovered, the secretary and armoire—mahogany, lemon wood, amaranth, gilded and patinated bronze, and white marble—are well known. Delivered on 5 December 1797 for the *hôtel* where Josephine and Napoleon lived on rue de la Victoire in Paris, the furnishings were soon thereafter transferred to Malmaison, and later brought to Munich by Prince Eugène after 1815; today they are at Nymphenburg castle.[9] The remainder of the room was decorated with a polished steel screen set in the fireplace, which Dubois, the master metalworker, had presented to

Bonaparte in 1800 when he passed through Dijon; a gilded bronze clock with a movement signed by Lepaute, damaged by the Prussians in 1815; two marble Medici vases; four smaller alabaster vases; and two sixteenth-century bronze statues from the school of Jean de Bologne, one representing Nessus and Dejanira, the other a horse. The room was lit by an ornate gilded bronze chandelier adorned with crystal. Only a few of the original paintings currently decorate the walls, including the portrait of Frederick the Great by Carteaux, which at the end of the First Empire replaced portraits of Madame (Josephine) Bonaparte painted by Gérard in 1801 (State Hermitage Museum, St. Petersburg) and Queen Hortense with her two sons by Madamoiselle Godefroid (Salon of 1812, now lost).

Dispersed at the sale of 1829, the Council Chamber's furniture was replaced by Napoleon III with pieces drawn from several imperial palaces. It is this grouping, joined by the original stools, that decorates the Salle du Conseil today. Together with a faithful restoration, the ensemble lends both an authentic quality and the charm of an occupied house to the château of Malmaison.

---

1. The etymology of the name "Malmaison" is disputed. The name may date back as far as the Norman invasion, when numerous battles were fought in the vicinity.

2. C. Percier and P.-F.-L. Fontaine, *Recueil de décorations intérieures comprenant tout ce qui a rapport à l'ameublement...* (Paris, 1801), pl. 55.

3. S. Grandjean, *Inventaire après décès de l'Impératrice Joséphine à Malmaison, 1814* (Paris, 1964), 95-96.

4. Archives nationales, Minutier central des notaires parisiens, LXVIII 832, 5 August 1824.

5. Archives nationales, Minutier central des notaires parisiens, LXVIII 867, 27 May 1829.

6. J. D. Passavant, ed., *Galerie Leuchtenberg, Gemälde Sammlung seiner Kaiserl. Hoheit des Herzogs von Leuchtenberg in München. In umrissen gestochen von inspector J. N. Muxel* (Frankfurt, 1851), pl. 262; and S.

Grandjean, "Un fauteuil napoléonien à la Malmaison," *Antologia di Belle Arti* 2 (1977): 201-02.

7. Paris, Place de la Bourse, Salle no. 2, Maîtres Bonnefons de Lavialle et Tournaire, sale on 23 and 24 April 1835, nos. 3 and 4.

8. The three original stools bear the stamp "Jacob Frères/rue Meslée" and a label "Salle du Conseil de Malmaison." Two (MM. 40.47.6961 and 6962) were acquired from Madame Engelman (20 July 1933) with a provenance from her ancestor, Madame Duplivissage, 18 rue de la Grande-Triperie, in Paris, who purchased them at the Malmaison auction in 1829. The third (MM.54.9.1) was acquired (1 July 1954) in the Parisian art market.

9. Wittelsbacher Ausgleichsfonds, M II c 23 for the secretary and M II a 26 for the armoire.

FIGURE 6

Jean-Auguste-Dominique Ingres, *Bonaparte as First Consul*, 1804,
Musée d'Art moderne et d'Art contemporain de la ville de Liège, on deposit at the Musée d'armes, Liège

FROM 𝒫ARIS TO 𝒫OINT ℬREEZE:

THE HISTORY OF NAPOLEON'S ARMCHAIR IN FRANCE AND AMERICA

ROBERTA J. M. OLSON *AND* MARGARET K. HOFER

PART I: 1800—1829

THE STORY OF the French armchair (*fauteuil*) central to this exhibition begins in Paris, France, in 1800 with the auspicious collaboration of three distinguished parties: the newly elected and power-hungry First Consul, Napoleon Bonaparte (1769–1821); the celebrated designers Charles Percier (1764–1838) and Pierre-François-Léonard Fontaine (1762–1853); and the era's leading French cabinetmaking firm, Jacob Frères (FIGURE 1).[1] Originally part of a suite of furniture that included ten armchairs, it is now the only surviving *fauteuil* from the group. The suite was commissioned by Napoleon for meetings of state in the Council Chamber (Salle du Conseil) on the ground floor of the country château of Malmaison (FIGURES 3 AND 4). This charming pastoral retreat about a half hour's ride west of Paris, site of the halcyon days of the Consulate, would become the favorite residence of Bonaparte's first consort and arbiter of fashion, Marie-Josèphe-Rose de Tascher de la Pagerie, widow de Beauharnais (1763–1814), whom he affectionately called "Josephine."

Percier and Fontaine—the renowned tastemakers and virtual creators of the Empire style, whose *à la mode* restoration Josephine had first seen at a neighbor's house in 1798—designed the Salle du Conseil and its furnishings. Their legendary meeting with Napoleon on 31 December 1799, recorded by Fontaine, occurred at the Luxembourg Palace, in Paris, where the

Bonapartes then resided.[2] Although the encounter was urged by the miniature painter Jean-Baptiste Isabey, the introductions were provided by the celebrated revolutionary painter Jacques-Louis David. As was his custom, Napoleon rudely ignored the newcomers for hours, although he did commission the partners to transform the dilapidated manor house as their maiden voyage under Napoleonic patronage. They worked on the refurbishment between 1800 and 1802 at a cost of well over 600,000 francs, raising the First Consul's ire and emptying his bank account. Nonetheless, Percier and Fontaine emerged from the commission as Napoleon's favored designers, their role intertwined with all official architectural and decorating projects of the head of state.[3]

A line engraving reproduced in the bible of the French Neoclassical style—Percier and Fontaine's *Recueil de décorations intérieures comprenant tout ce qui a rapport à l'ameublement* ("Collection of interior designs comprising everything that relates to furnishings")—preserves their design for the Salle du Conseil (FIGURE 5).[4] Fresh from studies in Rome, the pair adapted ancient Roman motifs and military references to serve both the fashion of the times and the image desired by their patron. Their success can be gauged by the fact that their efforts inspired all subsequent decoration of the palaces that Napoleon inhabited. The armchairs from this suite served as a template for many of the *fauteuils* acquired for the French residences of Bonaparte and his extended family, from the *hôtel* in the rue Cerrutti (1804–06) occupied by Napoleon's brother Prince Louis Bonaparte and Josephine's daughter Hortense de Beauharnais, to the later palace of Compiègne (1809). Napoleon embraced the iconography provided by Percier and Fontaine to further his own boundless political ambitions of empire, as discussed in the subsequent catalogue essay "The Empire Style as a Symbol of Power."

The inventory of Malmaison's contents made after Josephine's untimely death lists the original group of ten *grands fauteuils* and describes their decoration and upholstery.[5] The N-YHS chair and the rest of the suite in the Salle du Conseil remained at the château until 1829, when they were dispersed at the large auction of Malmaison furnishings held at the château. At that sale General Gourgaud (Baron Gaspard, 1783–1852), the Emperor's *aide-de-camp* who had accompanied him into his second and final exile on St. Helena, acquired two of the *fauteuils*, together with two stools in an X-shape (*tabourets en x*) and two sofas (*canapés* or *lits de repos*).[6] The latter four objects were subsequently sold by Gourgaud in Paris at an auction on 23–24 April 1835 at the Place de la Bourse.[7] After this time, all but two of the dispersed *fauteuils*, one of them the N-YHS armchair, disappeared from record.

While the Historical Society's armchair likely crossed the Atlantic soon after 1829, the only other securely recorded *fauteuil* from the suite was acquired sometime after the first Malmaison auction by Eugène Beauharnais (1781–1824), Josephine's son adopted by Napoleon, who transported it to Munich. Upon marrying the daughter of the King of Bavaria, Eugène settled at his father-in-law's court, where he became the Duke of Leuchtenberg. After its documentation at the Leuchtenberg Palace, in Munich, in a plate of a book published in 1851 (FIGURE 5), this second armchair

vanished from record.[8] According to a description of King Ludwig I of Bavaria, this chair—which had been used by Napoleon in his Malmaison "work room" until 1810—was treated like a cult relic and housed in a special shrinelike room, the *"Kabinet-Souvenir."*[9] King Ludwig also importantly noted that its arms bore marks made by Napoleon with a small knife.[10] Certainly this feature, not recorded in the 1851 illustration, increased the mythical status of the Leuchtenberg chair. Like the other eight *fauteuils* once decorating the Salle du Conseil, its disappearance and fate are shrouded in mystery, leaving the N-YHS armchair the lone survivor of the significant ensemble.

PART II: 1829–1867

Napoleon's *fauteuil* traversed the Atlantic to the adopted home of Napoleon's elder brother Joseph Bonaparte (1768–1844), known as the "gentle Bonaparte" (FIGURE 14). Appointed King of Naples (1806) by Napoleon and then proclaimed King of Spain (1808), Joseph fled France after Napoleon's defeat at Waterloo in 1815. Arriving in New York City under the alias of Monsieur Bouchard on 30 August 1815, Bonaparte tried in vain to conceal his identity. Within a week, however, the former King of Spain's arrival was trumpeted in the city's newspapers.[11]

The Count of Survilliers—as Joseph Bonaparte called himself in America—settled in Bordentown, New Jersey, at an elegant 1,800-acre estate on the Delaware River known as Point Breeze (FIGURE 7). Here he established himself in an exquisitely appointed mansion with magnificent collections of fine and decorative arts, entertaining other French émigrés and a host of wide-eyed American visitors in lavish style. His art collection, reportedly one of the finest in the country, introduced many Americans to European art and proved a significant catalyst in disseminating European

FIGURE 7

Charles B. Lawrence, *View from Bordentown Hill on the Delaware (Point Breeze)*, ca. 1820–30 (CHECKLIST NO. 14)

culture in America. Visitors to Point Breeze admired the monumental equestrian portrait *Napoleon Crossing the Alps* by David; works by old masters including Titian, Raphael, and Correggio; fine sculpture, furniture, silver, and porcelain; and an immense library rivaling the Library of Congress.[12] One Point Breeze guest wrote with astonishment in 1825, "a suite of rooms 15 ft. in [height] decorated with the finest productions of the pencils of Corego [sic]! Titian! Rubens! Vandyke! Vernet! Tenniers [sic] and Paul Potter and a library of the most splendid books I ever beheld."[13]

The exact date and circumstances of Joseph's acquisition of the *fauteuil* are uncertain. It may have been a gift from one of Napoleon's many devoted fol-

lowers who purchased souvenirs of the emperor at the Malmaison auction in 1829, such as General Gourgaud.[14] During his sojourns in England and on the Continent (1832–35, 1836–38), Joseph could also have acquired the chair through his own efforts. Napoleon's *fauteuil* most likely graced one of the main rooms of Point Breeze along with other mementos of the notorious emperor, including imposing portrait paintings by French masters, marble busts by Lorenzo Bartolini and Antonio Canova, and personal items used by Napoleon. Joseph's renowned art collection and cherished family mementos were undoubtedly concentrated at Point Breeze, his primary residence in America. In addition to Point Breeze, Joseph

FIGURE 8

Masthead of *Le Courrier des États-Unis*, 1828 (CHECKLIST NO. 29)

Bonaparte also kept a Philadelphia townhouse for the winter months and a summer retreat—of 26,000 acres—on the Black River in upstate New York.

At some point before his final departure for Europe in 1839, Joseph Bonaparte presented Napoleon's *fauteuil* to Félix Lacoste (1795–1853), a former officer in the French Imperial army and businessman with a trading company based in the former French colony of Santo Domingo. Lacoste and his wife, Emilie, came to New York in 1822, and the dashing young couple paid their first visit to Point Breeze in July 1823.[15] Joseph fell in love with the beautiful Emilie, and the Lacoste family subsequently moved into Point Breeze, with Emilie ostensibly serving as the companion to Bonaparte's young daughter Charlotte. In reality, Joseph Bonaparte kept Madame Lacoste as his mistress and fathered a son with her in 1825.[16] He arranged to have Félix Lacoste diverted, and conveniently absent, by reinvigorating Lacoste's Santo Domingo business with large sums of cash. He eventually appointed the unsuspecting Lacoste editor of his New York newspaper, *Le Courrier des États-Unis*, founded in 1828 (FIGURE 8).[17] Although no documentation for Joseph Bonaparte's gift of the chair to

Lacoste exists, Joseph is known to have presented Lacoste with a marble portrait bust of Napoleon by Canova and made numerous other gifts to friends and business associates.[18] It is probable that the chair was presented to Lacoste at the same time as the Canova bust, perhaps just before Joseph Bonaparte's final return to Europe in 1839.

Lacoste, separated from Emilie in 1828,[19] settled in New York City by 1831, and served as consul general of France in New York from 1850 until his death in 1853.[20] At the sale of his effects, the Napoleon *fauteuil* was acquired by Louis Borg (1812–after 1867), Lacoste's vice consul and his successor as consul general (1853–67). Upon Borg's return to France in 1867, he donated the history-laden *fauteuil* to the New-York Historical Society, then in its sixty-third year of operation.[21] A letter to the Society from Borg's agent, New York banker Archibald Gracie King (CHECKLIST NO. 35), declares Borg's wish to donate an "armchair in which Napoleon Bonaparte presided as First Consul of the Republic of France...brought from France by Joseph Bonaparte (Comte de Survilliers) given by him to Mr. Lacoste then French Consul at New York."[22]

Napoleon's chair was exhibited at the N-YHS during the late nineteenth century, but by the mid-twentieth century had been relegated to storage with other examples of then-unfashionable high-style European decorative arts. Curators rediscovered the *fauteuil* in the late 1980s at a time of renewed interest in the classical style. It was later included in the exhibition *Classical Taste in America 1800–1840*, organized by the Baltimore Museum of Art in 1993, interpreted as a seminal object in transmitting the Empire taste to America.[23] Now, 135 years after the *fauteuil's* deposit at the N-YHS, the *Seat of Empire* project is providing the first comprehensive analysis of the chair's physical structure and colorful history.

1. The firm was located in the rue Meslay, transcribed by them as "Meslée." For a genealogy and the various stamps of this family of furniture makers, see E. Dumonthier, *Les Sièges de Georges Jacob* (Paris, 1922), 9, or idem., *Sièges de Jacob Frères* (Paris, 1921), 10, updated by D. Ledoux-Lebard, *Le mobilier français du xixᵉ siècle, 1795–1889: dictionnaire des ébénistes et des menuisiers* (Paris, 1984, rev. ed. 1989), 268, within her consideration of the preeminent family firm (267–368). See also idem., *Les Ébénistes Parisiens (1795–1830)* (Paris, 1951), 133–57; H. Lefuel, *François-Honoré-Georges Jacob-Desmalter, ébéniste de Napoléon Ier et de Louis XVIII* (Paris, 1925); and S. Grandjean, *Empire Furniture 1800 to 1825* (New York, 1966), 35ff. The Jacob "dynasty" begun by Georges Jacob (1739–1814) was sold to his sons Georges (1768–1803) and François-Honoré-Georges Jacob (1776–1841), which from 1791 to 1803 carried the name Jacob Frères, after which François-Honoré changed the firm's name to Jacob-Desmalter & Cie.

2. The memorable accounts are recorded in both *Mia vita* (unpublished) and P.-F.-L. Fontaine, *Journal 1799–1853*, vol. 1 (Paris, 1987), 7 (in subsequent pages the architect discusses the embellishment of Malmaison and the individuals involved).

3. T. Wilson-Smith, *Napoleon and His Artists* (London, 1996), 101–02. For Percier and Fontaine, see: H. Ottomeyer, *Das frühe Oeuvre Charles Perciers (1782–1800). Zu den Anfängen des Historismus in Frankreich*, Ph.D. diss. Ludwig-Maximilians-Universität (Munich, 1981); idem., "Napoléon Bonapartes erste Möbel—das Hôtel de la Victoire und seine Ausstattung," *Kunst und Antiquitäten* 1/2 (1990): 26–35; and M. Culot, "Percier (-Bassant), Charles," and "Fontaine, Pierre-François-Léonard," *The Dictionary of Art*, vols. 24 and 7 (London, 1996), 387–89 and 256–59, respectively.

4. C. Percier and P.-F.-L. Fontaine, *Recueil de décorations intérieures comprenant tout ce qui a rapport à l'ameublement . . .* (Paris, 1801), pl. 55. For an illustration of the present state of the Salle du Conseil, which is scheduled for a more authentic restoration, together with a discussion of the room, see B. Chevallier, *Malmaison. Château et domaine des origines à 1904* (Paris, 1989), 158–60, fig. 71.

5. Inventory in the Archives nationales, Minutier central des notaires parisiens, LXVIII 776 and 781, 60, as transcribed in S. Grandjean, *Inventaire après décès de l'Impératrice Joséphine à Malmaison, 1814* (Paris, 1964), 96, no. 466: "Item deux lits de repos garnis de quatre carreaux de plumes, dix grands fauteuils, six chaises, dix X, le tout en bois bronzé et doré, foncés de crin et couverts de drap rouge, les X garnis d'une frange et d'un galon en or, un petit tabouret de pieds en pluche de soie, un tapis de vieille moquette, prisé le tout ensemble la somme de douze cents francs ci . . . . 1,200."

6. The sale of ten *fauteuils* in the suite from the Salle du Conseil is recorded in an annotated manuscript, "Vente mobilière de Malmaison," Archives nationales, Minutier central des notaires parisiens, LXVIII 867, which documents a sale beginning 31 May 1829 at which Gourgaud purchased nos. 495 and 496 for 78 and 70 francs, respectively (p. 35). The other eight *fauteuils* are cited on pp. 36, nos. 504, 507, 510; 40, no. 573; 42, nos. 593 (2), 594 (2). See also Grandjean, *Inventaire*, 96, n. 466.

7. Salle no. 2, Maîtres Bonnefons de Lavialle et Tournaire, nos. 3 and 4; see also ibid.

8. Reproduced on plate 262 in J. D. Passavant, ed., *Galerie Leuchtenberg. Gemälde Sammlung seiner Kaiserl. Hoheit des Herzogs von Leuchtenberg in München. In umrissen gestochen von inspector J. N. Muxel* (Frankfurt, 1851, with an 1852 English edition), in which it is identified as the *fauteuil* of the Emperor Napoleon. Andreas von Majewski, curator of the Wittels-bacher Ausgleichsfonds and the collections of the Duke of Bavaria, currently the owner of the palace (the Munich properties of the Leuchtenberg family were sold in 1854 to the Wittelsbach family), confirmed that the chair is not in the collections of the Duke of Bavaria. He also noted that there is no record of it in any of the inventories subsequent to the sale, suggesting that it remained with the Leuchtenberg family. The duke owns several other pieces of furniture with a Malmaison provenance; see H. Ottomeyer, "Möbel aus Malmaison in München," *Kunst und Antiquitäten* 3 (1990): 32–40. Members of the Leuchtenberg family whom the authors have contacted have no recollection of the armchair. See also S. Grandjean, "Un fauteuil napoléonien à la Malmaison," *Antologia di Belle Arti* 2 (1977): 201–02.

9. In Adalbert Prinz von Bayern, *Die Herzen der Leuchtenberg* (Munich, 1972), 271–72, as cited in Ottomeyer, "Möbel aus Malmaison": 39–40 and nn. 5, 24.

10. Ibid.; see also the subsequent catalogue essay "The Physical *Fauteuil*," n. 10.

11. *New-York Gazette*, 9 September 1815, 2, col. 1.

12. A. J. Bleecker, *Catalogue of Rare, Original Paintings . . . Valuable Engravings, Elegant Sculpture, Household Furniture . . . Belonging to the Estate of the Late Joseph Napoleon Bonaparte . . . to be sold . . . on Friday, June 25, 1847* (New York, 1847). The lot descriptions in this auction catalogue offer a vivid picture of Bonaparte's vast art collection. An earlier auction included the contents of Bonaparte's library; see T. Birch, Jr., *Catalogue of Valuable Books, Principally in the French Language, To Be Sold at Public Sale, on Thursday, September 18, 1845 . . .* (Philadelphia, 1845).

13. Letter of Reuben Haines 3 July 1825, quoted in P. T. Stroud, *The Emperor of Nature: Charles-Lucien Bonaparte and His World* (Philadelphia, 2000), 37.

14. See n. 6 above. Gourgaud was one of several loyal Bonapartists who discreetly purchased souvenirs of the emperor at the Malmaison auction.

15. G. Girod De L'Ain, *Joseph Bonaparte, Le Roi Malgré Lui* (Paris, 1970), 377–86. Girod De L'Ain's biography includes extensive description of the relationship between Joseph Bonaparte and Emilie Lacoste.

16. M. Ross, *The Reluctant King: Joseph Bonaparte, King of the Two Sicilies and Spain* (London, 1976), 262–63.

17. Ibid., 263.

18. E. M. Woodward, *Bonaparte's Park and the Murats* (Trenton, NJ, 1879), 67.

19. Girod De L'Ain, 382–86. Lacoste fought a duel with Emilie's subsequent lover, the author Prosper Mérimée, in January 1828, and the couple separated shortly thereafter. Joseph Bonaparte received unhappy letters from both Emilie and Félix, but judging from his kindly efforts on Félix's behalf, he sided with the cuckolded husband.

20. "Mort de M. Felix Lacoste, Consul Général de France," *Le Courrier des États-Unis*, 20 November 1853, 1.

21. Louis Borg divested himself of other historic treasures besides the *fauteuil*. Several weeks prior to his Historical Society donation, he sold his valuable collection of medals from his home on East 35th Street through a New York auction company. See H. H. Leeds & Miner, *Catalogue of the Well-Known Collection of Valuable Medals belonging to Mr. Louis Borg, Vice-Consul of France, who is about to be leaving for Europe* (New York, 1867). The majority of medals in Borg's collection were from the period of Napoleon's reign.

22. Minutes of the New-York Historical Society, 16 December 1867, N-YHS Archives.

23. W. A. Cooper, *Classical Taste in America 1800-1840*, exh. cat. (New York, 1993), 31.

FIGURE 9

Jacob Frères, Detail of armchair (*fauteuil*) from the Salle du Conseil at Malmaison, 1800 (CHECKLIST NO. 1)

THE $\mathcal{P}$HYSICAL $\mathcal{F}$AUTEUIL

ROBERTA J. M. OLSON *AND* MARGARET K. HOFER

THE HISTORICAL SIGNIFICANCE of the New-York Historical Society's Napoleonic *fauteuil* (FIGURE 1) is greatly enhanced by the integrity of the armchair's physical condition. Its gilded surface, underupholstery, showcover, and trim are all original, rendering this chair exceptionally rare and an important object for study. No other examples of documented Napoleonic furniture retain such extensive original material or provide such detailed physical information for studying and understanding the arts of French Empire cabinetmaking and upholstery.

The *fauteuil*'s massive frame is constructed of beech, a wood native to France whose hardness lends itself to carving.[1] A bold gold-on-black chromatic scheme, described in the 1814 Malmaison inventory as "*bronzé et doré*," adds to its commanding presence.[2] The term *bronzé* refers to the matte black paint (carbon black mixed with white lead pigment) that imitates the patina of oxidized ancient bronze, one of the chair's many references to the antique world. *Doré* describes the areas carved in relief and gilded in a traditional manner over a gesso base with the adhesive pigment red bole.[3] Carved and gilded areas include the chair's fluted stiles, whose sides are embellished with carved foliate scrolls (*rinceaux*) crowned by a rosette. Although the *fauteuil*'s frame does not bear a maker's mark, several other extant pieces from the Salle du Conseil are stamped by Jacob Frères.

The concave arm terminations of the *fauteuil* currently have gilt metal lion's-head masks, twenty-first-century reproductions that were cast from period examples, based on evidence of original mounts in that location.[4] The original mounts, probably made of gilded bronze, are discernible in two photographic negatives of the chair, the most recent dating from about 1936, in which it is seen that only one metal lion's-head mask on the proper left arm remains. The metal mounts that probably once embellished this armchair and the suite's other nine *fauteuils* appear in the unusual context of a painted and gilded frame. More typical of French furniture of the period are either gilded metal mounts attached to unpainted mahogany pieces or painted/gilded furniture with carved wooden embellishments. No exact correlation to the N-YHS *fauteuil* can be found among the slightly later models made for Napoleonic buildings by Jacob Frères or Jacob-Desmalter. Instead the arm terminations found on most of these chairs are either blank or feature gilded wood rosette attachments.[5] However, an exception occurs in the suite of gilded *fauteuils*, a variant model attributed to Jacob Frères, originally from the palace of Saint-Cloud, with gilded bronze rosettes attached via a metal pin.[6] Few of these slightly later *fauteuils* feature lions' heads in the arm terminations.[7] Since all of the later examples are entirely gilded, rendering them more opulent and less spartan, their

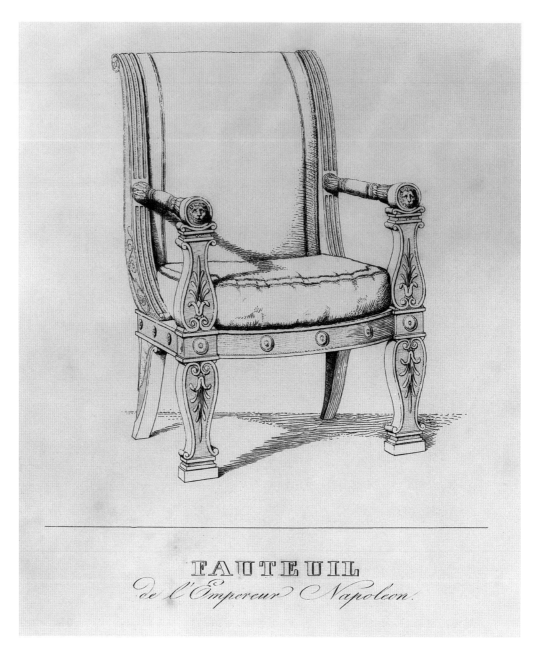

FAUTEUIL

de l'Empereur Napoléon.

FIGURE 10

Armchair from Malmaison at the Leuchtenberg Palace in Munich, plate 262 in *The Leuchtenberg Gallery*, 1852 (CHECKLIST NO. 33)

divergent color scheme underlines the singularity of the armchairs designed for the Salle du Conseil.

A weighing of the physical evidence seems to indicate that Percier and Fontaine intended metal mounts to embellish the *fauteuils* for the Council Chamber at Malmaison. Visible beneath the present mounts are three tiny telltale holes on each arm termination that have pierced the wood, testifying to the attachment of previous mounts.[8] Had the original mounts been made of wood, they most likely would have been attached via wood stanchions or a single metal pin. Wavy outlines of the lions' manes are also impressed into the paint surface of this area, suggesting that the original attachments were made of metal. Since the chair from the Salle du Conseil suite transported to Munich (FIGURE 10) had mounts identical to those of the N-YHS example, these were assuredly on the chairs when they resided at Malmaison prior to 1829. Most important, as recorded in their *Recueil* (FIGURE 5), Percier and Fontaine's highly integrated scheme for the Salle du Conseil featured many lions' heads as a theme with variations throughout the décor. The partners designed lion's heads on the legs of the central table (never executed), the panels covering the doors, and the medallions rhythmically punctuating the classical rail lining the walls. Behind the railing hung striped material simulating a military campaign tent that echoed the tentlike portico framing the courtyard entrance to the château (FIGURE 4).[9] In such a carefully coordinated room, it seems more than likely that Percier and Fontaine were responsible for the bronze mounts on the *fauteuils*. The question remains, do the mounts belong to the designers' original conception, or did Percier and Fontaine add them to harmonize with the décor of the room when the suite, fresh from the workshop of the Jacob Frères, was installed at Malmaison?

Physical evidence on the N-YHS *fauteuil* suggests that Napoleon himself actually may have used the chair. The top of the proper left (sitter's left) arm termination has a damaged area where the wood was weakened and subsequently chipped off. Napoleon was left-handed, and reportedly, in his hallmark impatience (he considered 15 minutes for a state dinner the absolute maximum), habitually drummed on objects with a knife. In addition, King Ludwig I reputedly described the Munich *fauteuil* as having been cut on the arms by Napoleon with a penknife, not visibly apparent in the 1851 engraving representing that lost chair (FIGURE 10).[10] These tantalizing marks of history seem to preserve tangible proof of Napoleon's notorious impatience inflicted on the lone surviving *fauteuil* from the Salle du Conseil.

Amazingly the *fauteuil* retains all its original upholstery components after more than two hundred years. The chair's upholstery is made up of multiple components, typical of French upholstery practices of the period. A wooden seat frame attaches the under-upholstery to the chair's inner rails; webbing made from bast (a fibrous plant material) and a thin layer of hair provides support for the seat cushion; a deck cloth of bleached bast covers the webbing; and a loose hair-filled seat cushion retaining its original form, square profile, and notched corners sits on top of the deck. The seat-cushion filling is stitched to compress the hair and covered with a later bleached bast filler cover.

The visible components of the *fauteuil*'s upholstery include a red showcover made from heavily napped plain-weave wool, echoing the red wool fringe (*franges*) on the striped fabric lining the walls of the Salle du Conseil. Dye analysis of the showcover fabric revealed the use of cochineal, a dye made from the bodies of a tropical insect (*Dactylopius coccus*), to achieve a vivid red color. The trim outlining the seat back, outback, cushion, and *manchettes* (arms) is composed of gilded silver thread with black velvet ribbon, a color scheme that echoed the gold and black of the seat frame.[11] A good portion of the trim is missing from the seat and arms, leaving a shadow of its original outline, and the seat-back trim has some losses. Upholstery analysis revealed that the showcover, though original, may have been removed, reconfigured, and reattached at some point during the late nineteenth or early twentieth centuries.[12] The heavy soiling of the showcover, possibly a result of exposure to a coal-fired furnace, is not further reversible without disassembly of the upholstery components.

The *fauteuil*'s condition presented a dilemma to the Historical Society's staff. Curators agreed that preservation of the original materials was of utmost importance. On the other hand, the chair's soiled upholstery and aged gilding made it difficult for a general audience to appreciate its original brilliance. To address this challenge, the N-YHS adopted a two-part conservation strategy: traditional conservation treatments aimed at stabilizing its fragile surfaces, followed by the application of digital technology to virtually "restore" the chair to its original condition (FIGURE 2). Digital photographs of the chair were carefully enhanced to clean and brighten the red showcover, enliven the gilding, and replace lost areas of trim. Visitors to the exhibition will view the actual Napoleon armchair adjacent to a projected image of a life-size, rotating virtual *fauteuil*, digitally renewed to its original splendor.[13]

---

1. Pascale Patris performed the treatments on the wood surfaces. Wood identification (*Fagus spp.*) was based on microanalysis performed in 2001. The chair was stabilized prior to its exhibition at the Baltimore Museum of Art in 1993, with treatments performed at the Museum of American Textile History, in North Andover, Massachusetts, and at the Society for the Preservation of New England Antiquities conservation facility in Waltham, Massachusetts.

2. S. Grandjean, *Inventaire après décès de l'Impératrice Joséphine à Malmaison, 1814* (Paris, 1964), 96, no. 466, fully quoted in the preceding catalogue essay "From Paris to Point Breeze," n. 5.

3. The gilding is abraded in many areas so that red bole, and in some cases the gesso layer, is visible. Only in narrow overlapping areas are traces of red bole found under the black pigment, proving that gilding was planned for specified areas and applied before the black paint.

4. The source of the replacement mounts is P. E. Guerin Inc., a New York City fine hardware supplier since 1857 with samples dating back to early nineteenth century. The *fauteuil*'s mounts had been lost by the time of its 1993 exhibition in Baltimore and were replaced by stamped metal copies, whose diameters were smaller than the originals.

5. Those with plain terminations include examples at: the Mobilier national, Paris, attributed to Jacob Frères (Musée municipal de Saint-Cloud, *Napoléon Bonaparte à Saint-Cloud: du coup d'etat de brumaire a la fin de l'empire*, exh. cat. [Saint-Cloud, 1999], 82, nos. 116-17); Fontainebleau, a variant model with the stamp of Jacob Frères (E. Dumonthier, *Sièges de Jacob Frères* [Paris, 1921], 40); Fontainebleau, a different variant model with the stamp of Jacob Frères and a provenance from General Moreau (Musée national du château de Fontainebleau, *Un ameublement à la mode en 1802: le mobilier du General Moreau*, exh. cat., ed. by J.-P. Samoyault and C. Samoyault Verlet [Paris, 1992], 38–39, no. 30, fig. 30a); Drouot, Paris, sale cat. (30/V/90), lot 163, probably with the stamp of Jacob-Desmalter; Christie's, London, sale cat. (12/IV/84), lot 66, with the stamp of Jacob-Desmalter, repeated in Christie's, London, sale cat. (12/XII/96), lot 180, from the *hôtel* of Hortense de Beauharnais and Louis Napoleon in the rue Cerrutti, one with the stamp of Jacob-Desmalter; Paris, private collection, four, one with the stamp of Jacob-Desmalter, that were part of a suite with two *bergères* and a sofa, with a provenance from the Grand Salon de Reception of Prince Louis. Those with rosettes in the arm terminations include examples at: the Palais Royal, Brussels, a variant model attributed to Jacob Frères with a provenance from the Salon de Musique at Saint-Cloud (Musée national du château de Fontainebleau, *Un ameublement*, 38–39, no. 30, unnumbered fig., whose *tabourets* in the same suite have lions' heads at the center of the x); Compiègne, a variant model with the stamp of Jacob-Desmalter (S. Grandjean, *Empire Furniture 1800 to 1825* [New York, 1966], fig. 49a, and P. Kjellberg, *Le meuble français et européen du moyen âge a nos jours* [Paris, 1991], fig. 491 caption); Christie's, Monaco, sale cat. (14/XII/96), lot 118, with the stamp of Jacob-Desmalter.

6. Today in the Palais Royal, Brussels: see Musée national du château de Fontainebleau, *Un ameublement*, 38–39, no. 30, unnumbered fig.

7. Most similar to the Malmaison *fauteuils* (save their overall gilding) are a pair with the stamp of Jacob-Desmalter from the *hôtel* of Hortense de Beauharnais and Louis Napoleon in the rue Cerrutti (Christie's, London, sale cat. [12/XII/96], lot 179). When contacted by the auction house on behalf of the N-YHS, the purchaser did not confirm whether the mounts were made of wood or metal. From a photograph, only one lion's head remains; two of the other three terminations betray a residue of material in the area and one a stanchion. A pair of nearly identical *bergères* with the stamp of Jacob-Desmalter, the same early provenance from the *hôtel* in the rue Cerrutti, and lions' heads in gilded wood at the arm terminations were brought to our attention by François Fabius (Gallerie Koller, Zürich, sale cat. [2-6/X/01], lot 1263).

8. Most likely after the original nails loosened, screws were used to attach the mounts (a frequent occurrence in furniture of the period). Two

screws, in fact, remain pounded in the wood, and two of the three holes on the proper right reveal traces of screw grooves.

9. Grandjean, *Inventaire*, 95, no. 463, notes that the room, which took ten days to install in the form of a tent, is described in the 1812 edition of the *Recueil*. See also B. Chevallier, *Malmaison, Château et domaine des origines à 1904* (Paris, 1989), 92 and 158, who notes that after her divorce from Napoleon, Josephine kept this room intact. For Napoleon's actual striped tent (1808), see idem., *Napoleon*, exh. cat., trans. T. M. Gunther (Memphis, 1993), 146, no. 170.

10. H. Ottomeyer, "Möbel aus Malmaison in München," *Kunst und Antiquitäten* 3 (1990): 39, cites Adalbert Prinz von Bayern, *Die Herzen der Leuchtenberg* (Munich, 1972), 271–72: "Ein Sessel aus Napoleons Arbeitzimmer in Malmaison, dessen er sich bis 1810 bedient, was meine Augen bei Staatsratssitzungen gesehen. Daß er mit einem Fed-ermesser die Arme seines Sessls schnitt, ist auch an diesem zu bemerken." Chevallier, *Malmaison*, 159, notes that the Munich chair was used by Napoleon to preside over the council at Malmaison and that it "était marqué de coups de canif."

11. It is significant that across the vestibule on the ground floor of Malmaison, in the Salon de Musique, the suite of furniture (mahogany frames with gilded elements) by Jacob Frères had a harmonizing red upholstery with black trim, as preserved in a watercolor by Auguste Garnerey (1785–1824); Grandjean, *Inventaire*, pl. III; and F. Baudot, *Style Empire* (Paris, 1999), 24–25, 76 (in color). This high degree of decorative coordination is important in reconstructing the N-YHS Napoleon chair within its original setting.

12. Nancy C. Britton performed the upholstery analysis and treatment.

13. Digital technology designer Han Vu created the virtual restoration.

FIGURE 11

Gobelins, Atelier of Pierre-François Cozette, after Gérard, Tapestry: *Napoleon I in His Coronation Robes*, 1808–11 (CHECKLIST NO. 19)

THE EMPIRE ARMCHAIR AS A SYMBOL OF POWER

ROBERTA J. M. OLSON

SINCE ANCIENT TIMES the impressive chair or throne has been emblematic of political or religious rank and authority, and Napoleon Bonaparte, a brilliant military strategist and political opportunist, seized upon this age-old symbol to legitimize his own rise to power. As Napleon's "star," which he claimed guided his every move, ascended in the political firmament, the chairs he commissioned for his residences, as well as those depicted in portraits of him, reflected the self-image he wished to promulgate via these propaganda furnishings. "A King does not exist in nature," Bonaparte wrote, "he exists only in civilization: there cannot be a King *simple*, he is only a King when dressed."[1] Napoleon did not so much vault onto the imperial throne as move steadily, albeit swiftly, toward dictatorship. Each assertion of new powers came gilded with a veneer of legality and a rhetorical commitment to the principles of 1789, hedging against any resurgent Jacobin radicalism like that which had engineered the coup that brought him to power. Until Napoleon's luck changed and his health declined, his meteoric rush to empire can be charted in the chairs that populated his various residences and portraits. As he altered fashion and taste to suit his goals, with the sophisticated help of tastemakers Percier and Fontaine, the chair functioned as an enduring device of statecraft in a heady mix of power, politics, and style.

A foreigner from Corsica who ironically spoke with a pronounced accent and wrote poorly in French, Napoleone Buona Parte (his original Italian name) fulfilled the French need for an executive figure to fill the unstable vacuum left in the wake of the Reign of Terror (1793–95).[2] He captured the imagination of the masses, exhausted by the excesses of the French Revolution, and passionately manipulated the means to power with speed and agility, a process amounting to one of the greatest acts of political seduction ever recorded.[3]

The French Revolution evolved in several political stages, each with a different style of governing that lent their respective names to periods in the decorative arts, all being subsumed under the generic umbrella term "Empire style." The first phase under the revolutionary government (1789–95) was followed by the Directory (1795–99). This in turn was quickly superceded by the Consulate (1799–1804), based roughly on a Roman model, wherein Napoleon served as First Consul. When Bonaparte crowned himself emperor in Notre Dame Cathedral in 1804, he initiated the full-blown Empire style, which proved more successful than his political empire.[4]

Since the "Napoleon armchair" (FIGURES 1, 9, 13, 18), commissioned in 1800 on the design of Percier and Fontaine and made by the firm of Jacob Frères, belongs to the Consulate phase of the Empire style, its style can be referred to as Consular or Consulate. Its forms clearly expressed the ideals not only of Napoleon but also of this phase of the French Revolution, just as the distinctive Directoire style—epitomized by the furniture of Georges Jacob, the father of the Jacob brothers—embodied those of the Directory. During the Consular period, furniture featured more defined silhouettes and controlled symmetry in decoration than in the Directory, characteristics that endured into the mature Empire style, albeit with a more pronounced imperial grandeur.

The Empire style belongs to a larger, complex cultural trend toward classical forms called Neoclassicism.[5] Already by the middle of the eighteenth century and prior to the French Revolution, simpler, more sober classical forms had begun to replace the extravagantly sinuous forms of the Rococo style. Fed by Enlightenment ideals and experiences of individuals returning from the Grand Tour, the frivolity of the Rococo became linked to the *ancien régime*, the Bourbon monarchy, whereas the new, more stoical style heralded revolutionary thoughts. This reaction found its artistic and theoretical focus in a re-evaluation of the legacy of classical antiquity, of both the glory that was Greece and the grandeur that was Rome. The emerging style was fueled by the first organized excavations of the ruins in the Italian resort town of Herculaneum on the Gulf of Naples near Pompeii, which began in 1738 and whose discoveries were spread by sumptuously illustrated books with reliable archaeological information. Although excavators had unearthed examples of ancient furniture at Herculaneum and Pompeii, such as the well-known bronze tables, the new breed of designers was more affected by large numbers of recently discovered wall paintings. Among the multiple influences operative during the early days of this essentially romantic style were the prints of Giovanni Battista Piranesi, whose fresh

interpretations of the antique are credited as strong influences on Percier and Fontaine, the designers of the N-YHS armchair. A rich background of archaeology as well as visual and verbal theory, as found in the writings of Johann Joachim Winckelmann, lay behind Neoclassicism's long-lived international period of influence (1760–1830).

This renewed perception of the ancient world became increasingly important to furniture designers as they strove to keep in tune with the currents of the times by creating ever-more faithful interpretations of antiquity. After 1789 an increasingly austere version of Neoclassicism developed in France, driven by politics and the excitement about its stylistic implications. Similar attitudes find reflection in the forms of the N-YHS *fauteuil*, which fully expresses the Empire style in its Consulate incarnation. With the official creation of the Empire in 1804, the style became more ornate and imperial. Its impact proved to be enormous as it spread throughout Europe in the wake of Napoleon's conquests, accelerated by the installation of Bonaparte family members as ruling regional monarchs.

The accession of Bonaparte as First Consul in 1799 (named First Consul for life in 1802) initiated the revival of official state patronage and the recovery of the French furniture trade as a new consumer economy swept France. Napoleon was, to a large degree, responsible for restoring the decorative arts to their preeminent position among the arts of France. The most influential designers of the Consulate and mature Empire periods were none other than Napoleon's official architects Percier and Fontaine, who, during their extensive travels in Italy, had studied not only the ruins of antiquity but also Renaissance-era *palazzi*. Under the patronage of Napoleon's fashionable consort, Josephine, the taste-making pair became the most important decorators in France, reinterpreting the magnificence and grace of ancient styles to suit their modern needs. Josephine's small leased house in the rue Chantereine (renamed the rue de la Victoire) was stylistically one of their most successful projects, followed in the early 1800s by the exquisitely planned interiors at Malmaison.[6]

The heavy rectangular form of N-YHS's majestic *fauteuil* is typical of the weighty grandeur of the Consulate and early Empire styles. Every detail reflects General Bonaparte's political goals, his physical person, and his personality. Its low seat was especially suitable for the ruler's short stature (his exact height is unknown, although most estimates place it around 5 feet, 2 inches). The massive proportions of the *fauteuil* compensated for Napoleon's diminutive form, endowing its sitter with a confident majesty. The chair's bold red, black, and gold color scheme was repeated in other pieces of furniture for the Salle du Conseil, such as the *tabourets* (FIGURE 12),[7] a color conceit tied to the general's and his architects' visions of ancient Roman power.

More specifically the chair's form reflects the simple but heavy "martial" style that came into vogue during the Directory. Some examples of this military-style furniture, replete with martial symbols, have sober black and gold accents.[8] After Napoleon's intoxicating victories in the Italian campaign, Percier and Fontaine—attempting to create an appropriate conjugal setting for the nation's hero—had designed a military-style bedchamber for the Hôtel de la Victoire in which the beds were painted to resemble antique bronze.[9] Napoleon felt so comfortable in a militaristic environment that it seemed natural he live like a soldier at home. Precedents for the chromatic combination of gold and black existed in earlier French cabinetmaking, in ebony-veneered pieces with gilded bronze and in black lacquer and gilt pieces with a decided Chinese or Japanese influence, in vogue from the time of Louis XV.[10] Of course, the impact of Napoleon's Corsican ancestry and his ties with Italy, freshly in his mind from

FIGURE 12

Jacob Frères, Stool (*tabouret*) from the Salle du Conseil at Malmaison, 1800 (CHECKLIST NO. 2)

the Italian campaign and therefore rekindled in the minds of his designers, remained pivotal to the style and colors created for the *fauteuils* in the Salle du Conseil.[11] Throughout his reign, Napoleon manifested a taste for things Italian in culture as well as politics, from ancient Rome to contemporary artists like Andrea Appiani and Antonio Canova.[12]

In contrast to the overt symbols of the French Revolution during the 1790s, such as the tricolor cockade, the iconography of N-YHS's armchair and its motifs evoked antiquity via a contemporary design that was cutting-edge for its day. Its austere forms developed from the *style étrusque* (Etruscan style), an avant-garde Neoclassical mode of the late 1780s, in an

FIGURE 13

Jacob Frères, Armchair (*fauteuil*) from the Salle du Conseil at Malmaison, 1800 (CHECKLIST NO. 1)

attempt to ally the fledgling French Republic in its Consulate manifestation with the virtuous Roman Republic. Janus-faced elements of the armchair also anticipated the opulence of the later Empire, notably its gilding, a universal symbol of wealth and glory. The chair's color scheme abounds with references to the Graeco-Roman world. After all, red and black were the basic colors of ancient Greek vases, collected assiduously by savvy Etruscans and early Romans, and the red of the chair's upholstery approximates the famous Pompeiian red hue of frescos that had been unearthed in the shadow of Vesuvius. Above all, red was the color of sovereign power among the Romans, underlining the *fauteuil*'s political allusions.[13]

The chair's individual carved motifs present a veritable primer in the eclectic vocabulary of ancient decorative symbols. In aggregate, these motifs boasted the martial success and power of the First Consul, qualities that promised prosperity and identified France with the military prowess of the Roman Empire. The chair's arms are each carved with three bands of stylized laurel leaves, signifying victory and triumph and arranged to vaguely resemble the shape of a lotus flower.[14] These leaves, like several other motifs on the *fauteuil*, were echoed in the décor of its setting, the Salle du Conseil (FIGURE 5). Its arms rest on baluster-shaped supports whose Roman-inspired carved palmettes allude to military victory and fame, the sequel to victory.[15] These supports are echoed in mirror images on the two front legs to form double balusters, each bisected by the front seat rail embellished with a carved and gilded sacrificial (or sacral) plate, a trophy of war emblematic of triumph.[16] The double balusters, resembling two candelabra or vases, are each crowned by a volute forming the upper section of a diminutive iconic capital, whose base, the abacus, is punctuated by a flower. The armchair's rear legs are raked to recall the saberlike forms of the quintessential Neoclassical fur-

niture form, the *klismos* chair. Stylized gilded wings, another ancient victory symbol, decorate the lateral profiles of the armchair's rear legs,[17] and foliate or acanthus scrolls (*rinceaux*) embellish the sides of the classically fluted chair stiles (FIGURE 13). On the outside flank of each stile the scrolling termination encloses a rosette, a motif repeated inside the lower tendril of the foliate scroll. Both the foliate arabesques and the rosettes make subtle reference to prosperity and fecundity.[18] What is more, the scrollwork is archaeologically accurate and closely approximates stucco examples on the vault of the mausoleum of the Valerii in the via Latina, Rome.[19] Decorating the slightly bowed front seat rail are three additional sacral plates, a motif that continues around the armchair in a friezelike fashion for a total of seventeen (FIGURES 13, 18). Finally, the lion's-head mounts of the Society's armchair also derive from Roman models.[20] Considered as a whole, the decorative ornaments of N-YHS's *fauteuil* achieve a balance between the sober austerity of a republican style and the imperial connotations of Neoclassicism referencing past glories and potential splendor.

In addition to the military allusions found in the N-YHS *fauteuil* and Napoleon's Salle du Conseil, the chair's red upholstery and contrasting tailored trim recall a military uniform. The painstakingly constructed black velvet, silk, and gilded silver trim creates an effect similar to the tailored costume of a uniformed officer. Even the choice of a heavily napped wool, as opposed to a luxurious silk, suggests the practical aspects of military dress in keeping with the republicanism of the Napoleonic myth.

Although the armchair—destined for the private, elite sphere of Bonaparte's cabinet meetings in the Salle du Conseil of his country residence—was never intended for public display, its general symbolism would have been understood by the average French citizen. The classical symbolism of the chair's architectural style was immediately accessible, since classical imagery had already permeated popular culture and the decorative and fine arts in France (for example, the Pantheon, by Jacques-Germain Soufflot, 1755–92). Under Napoleon, classical ideas found their most momumental public expression in two permanent structures: Pierre Vignon's "temple of glory" La Madeleine (1807–42) and Percier and Fontaine's Arc du Carrousel (1806–08), designed on the model of the Arch of Constantine, in Rome. In 1800, the year of the armchair's commission, Napoleon was the man of the hour, and the French citizenry was ecstatic over his victories and enthralled with the classicizing dress and furnishings of his modish consort. French citizens would have grasped the chair's military allusions, since culture of the time was saturated with martial imagery and the splendid regalia of the French army. Above all, the French public could not have failed to be impressed by the *fauteuil*'s magnificence, one of the primary qualities Napoleon employed throughout his reign to woo the masses. Because of its familiar vocabulary, this type of *fauteuil* was a frequently used prop in the visual arts.

Napoleon instinctively understood the power of propaganda in art and fashion, using it to forge a correlation between Caesar and his own public image, and between the ancient Roman and the new French Republics. The authoritative N-YHS armchair, one of many propagandist tools he deployed in constructing that imagery, functioned as the stylish symbol of the First Consul's power. Later, as Bonaparte's power grew more absolute, the chairs he commissioned became more elegant, imperial luxury itself making a political statement. Eventually the *fauteuil* form gave way to a throne, as depicted in a tapestry portrait of Emperor Napoleon after a painting, known in multiple versions, by François-Pascal-Simon Baron Gérard (FIGURE 11).[21] Thus, the iconography of N-YHS's armchair is

transitional, midway between the more republican sentiments of the French Revolution and the absolute power of the Empire, when a crowned Napoleon was frequently depicted seated on or standing near a throne, as in portraits by Jean-Auguste-Dominique Ingres and Gérard. Although an armchair is emblematic of power, it suggests less overt authority than an imperial throne, alluding instead to diplomacy, negotiations, and writing, all tools of statecraft. Moreover, its arms connote stability and balance, qualities desperately needed in France after the political upheavals of the 1790s. As a type, the armchair served as one of the most prominent rhetorical symbols of Napoleonic visual propaganda during the middle years of his career.

In the past, the Society's armchair has been associated with a number of Empire chairs recorded in portraits and other representations of Bonaparte, most dating to the early years of his power, by assorted Napoleonic artists.[22] While not identical to any of these, it is closely related in type to several of the armchairs depicted and in symbolism to all of them. First and foremost among the group is Ingres's state portrait *Napoleon as First Consul*, painted in 1804 for the town of Liège in Belgium to assert the legitimacy of Napoleon's rule (FIGURE 6). Since the rising artistic star Ingres never visited Liège, the *fauteuil*, which functions as a chair of office, may have been an amalgamation of chairs the artist had seen, or a studio prop.[23] The featured chair is a variant of the Jacob Frères prototype from the Salle du Conseil. Clearly constructed of unpainted mahogany and decorated with gilded metal mounts, it—like the N-YHS chair—has lion's-head masks in the arm terminations. Since none of these embellishments are military in nature, Ingres's emphasis in the portrait is on the civilian nature of Napoleon's role, which is echoed in the civilian red costume with its gold-embroidered trim that Bonaparte wears.[24] As with the Society's armchair, this *fauteuil* reinforces the First Consul's power.

Similar armchairs were included in works of art even more obviously animated by political propaganda. For example, a drawing attributed to Gérard, *The Signing of the Concordat between France and the Papacy on 16 July 1801* (CHECKLIST NO. 8), depicts the First Consul seated on a *fauteuil* nearly identical to N-YHS's chair, even down to its lion's-head mounts.[25] It is noteworthy that everyone in the composition, save Bonaparte, is standing. Napoleon, positioned at the center of the composition about to place his signature on the momentous political document that reinstated Catholicism as the religion of the majority of French people, clearly holds the reins of power. His authority is bolstered by the solidity and strength of the majestic *fauteuil*, clearly dominant over the other prominent chair in the drawing, a side chair without arms (*chaise*). At royal residences, the design and materials of chairs usually served to place the sitters in ranking order, with armchairs reserved for the individuals of the highest authority. Even before the onset of his reign as emperor, Napoleon and his propaganda machine had adopted this protocol.[26]

In later paintings, like David's *Napoleon in His Study* (1812), the chair model evolved into a more elegant type characteristic of the mature Empire style.[27] Yet in each of these carefully choreographed interior scenes Napoleon, the military genius, is shown engaged in implied acts of statecraft, as opposed to earlier portraits stressing his military accomplishment—notably David's dramatic equestrian portrait *Napoleon Bonaparte Crossing the Alps by the Great Saint Bernard Pass* (1801), as well as Gros's *Napoleon Bonaparte at the Bridge of Arcole* (1796) and his *Bonaparte Visiting the Plague-Stricken Soldiers in the Hospital at Jaffa* (1804)[28]— where the general's heroic stance is more active.

Close political associates and Bonaparte family members were also aggrandized in portraits that incorporated chairs similar to the N-YHS *fauteuil*.

Arguably among the most beautiful is Gérard's portrayal of Michel, Count Regnaud de Saint-Jean d'Angély (1808), a crucial ally of Napoleon who served as secretary of state in 1807 and as a witness to the Bonaparte divorce (CHECKLIST NO. 12).[29] The frame of its *fauteuil* departs from the model of the N-YHS armchair only in its overall gilding and the absence of lion's-head mounts. Just as David had commissioned chairs from Georges Jacob to use for Napoleon and other sitters,[30] Gérard may have owned a similar *fauteuil*, which he included in many portraits of the Bonaparte clan as emblematic of Napoleonic power.[31]

The earlier *fauteuil* model by Jacob Frères, as represented by the Historical Society's armchair, was utilized in the consular palaces of Malmaison and Saint-Cloud (1801–02). Variants of this prototype were produced for the imperial palaces—such as Rambouillet, Laeken, and Compiègne—by the firm's later incarnation, Jacob-Desmalter, sometimes on the order of the *Garde-meuble* (the office responsible for furnishing Napoleon's residences). Other members of the court also commissioned analogous ensembles, for example, those with a provenance from the Second Consul, Jean-Jacques-Regis de Cambacérès, and those from the Parisian *hôtel* of Napoleon's brother Prince Louis Bonaparte and Hortense de Beauharnais.[32]

As the Empire style and Napoleon's dominion spread abroad, this type of *fauteuil* enjoyed an international cachet, with occasional adaptations to local taste.[33] (For a discussion of the dissemination of the style in America, see the subsequent catalogue essay "Empire Abroad: The French Taste in New York, 1800–1840.") Scholars have viewed the Society's historic armchair, formerly belonging to Joseph Bonaparte, as influential in spreading the Empire style on this side of the Atlantic.[34]

One of several fine examples of the French Empire style in the collections of the New-York Historical

Society, the Napoleon armchair is usually displayed in the new Henry Luce III Center for the Study of American Culture adjacent to a side chair of Louis XVI commissioned by his queen, Marie Antoinette.[35] This juxtaposition of two significant seats—a *chaise* of the Bourbon monarchy and an armchair of the French Revolution's latter-day hero and later emperor—forms an ironic historical confrontation, revealing the transient nature of political power. These two magnificent seats bracket a crucial period in French history, encompassing the French monarchy, the Revolution that resulted in the overthrow of that monarchy, and Napoleon's rise as First Consul. It is telling that these

potent symbols of European empires found their way to the young United States, whose revolution had fed that of France and resulted in a country founded on democratic principles. It seems especially appropriate that they now reside at the New-York Historical Society, whose collection of paintings includes the landmark five-part allegorical series by Thomas Cole, *The Course of Empire* (1833–36), documenting the rise and inevitable fall of all empires ruled by despots. In its New York setting, Bonaparte's majestic armchair remains a seminal document of the Napoleonic era and an enduring polemical symbol of political power.

---

1. Quoted in P. Lewis and G. Darley, *Dictionary of Ornament* (New York, 1986), 121.

2. The emergence of Napoleon, and his later resurrection of a hereditary monarchy presided over by a dictator, was not so different from the Bourbon monarchy that preceded him. See I. Woloch, *Napoleon and His Collaborators. The Making of a Dictatorship* (New York, 2001). See also Grand Palais, Paris, *Napoléon*, exh. cat. (Paris, 1969).

3. In her memoirs Josephine's daughter Hortense commented: "My stepfather is a comet of which we are but the tail; we must follow him without knowing where he carries us—for our happiness or for our grief." Quoted by E. Bruce, *Napoleon and Josephine: An Improbable Marriage* (New York, 1995), 328. Bonaparte's political career was marred by his selective historical amnesia and hubris.

4. For a discussion of the transformations in the furniture trades and styles during this period, see L. Auslander, *Taste and Power: Furnishing Modern France* (Berkeley, 1992), 147–59.

5. See H. Honour, "Neo-Classicism," in the Arts Council of Great Britain, *The Age of Neo-Classicism*, exh. cat. (London and Harlow, 1972), xxi–xxix, together with the other essays and entries.

6. See C. Payne, ed., *Sotheby's Concise Encyclopedia of Furniture* (London, 1989), 81–91. The entire July 1977 issue of *Apollo* (106: 185) contains informative articles about Josephine's distinguished patronage and much-lauded taste.

7. Malmaison currently has three *tabourets en x* with a provenance from the Salle du Conseil with the stamp of Jacob Frères, as well as two from state bedroom of Joachim Murat at the Elysée Palace without a stamp, all with replacement showcovers.

8. For example, A. Forray-Carlier, *Le Mobilier du Musée Carnevalet* (Dijon, 2000), 219, no. 82, reproduces a commode, enhanced by Roman *fascies* at its corners, in the "martial" style. Made in Paris ca. 1795, it has areas painted to simulate both black patinated and gilded bronze.

9. For a reconstruction of the room (ca. 1796–97), draped to resemble a striped tent with furniture and accoutrements in a military vocabulary,

see H. Ottomeyer, "Napoléon Bonapartes erste Möbel—das Hôtel de la Victoire und seine Ausstattung," *Kunst und Antiquitäten* 1/2 (1990): 33–34, fig. 12. For the bed, see Archives nationales, Paris, *Napoléon tel qu'en lui-même*, exh. cat. (Paris, 1969), 32, no. 79.

10. See P. Hughes, *The Wallace Collection. Catalogue of Furniture*, vol. 2 (London, 1996), 541–46, no. 119; 546–53, no. 120, among others, and especially 1114–19, no. 219, a pair of French tables (1785–87) with a gilt-bronze frieze over black painted steel panels; and Forray-Carlier, 64–65.

11. For pertinent Italian examples, see A. González-Palacios, *I mobili italiani: il patrimonio artistico del Quirinale* (Milan, 1996), 188–210; 292–93, no. 110; and P. Rosazza Ferrara, *Il Museo Mario Praz* (Rome, 1991), 35–36, who reproduces a black painted and gilded classicizing wall console (*mensola*). See also E. Colle, *Il mobile Impero in Italia: arredi e decorazioni d'interni dal 1800 al 1843* (Milan, 1998), 36–37, no. 2; 38–39, no. 3; 110–11, no. 25; and Palazzo Reale, Milan, *Il Neoclassicismo in Italia da Tiepolo a Canova*, exh. cat. (Milan, 2002), 231, 478, no. VIII.12, a wall table of Roman manufacture before 1777.

12. See J.-M. Olivesi, "Le goût italien de l'Empereur des Français," in Musée Fesch, Ajaccio, *Napoleon, les Bonaparte et l'Italie*, exh. cat. (Ajaccio, 2001), 6–11; and F. Haskell and N. Penny, *Pour l'amour de l'Antique* (Paris, 1999).

13. G. Ferguson, *Signs and Symbols in Christian Art* (London, 1954), 152.

14. Ibid., 33; and J. Hall, *Dictionary of Signs and Symbols in Art* (New York, 1974; rev. ed. 1979), 190, who notes that the small-leaved *Laurus nobilis*, the bay, was used to make the victor's crown. The plant was also thought to have prophylactic qualities.

15. Ferguson, 36; and Hall, 231.

16. These Roman sacrificial plates appear as architectural decoration on friezes, triumphal arches, and altars. In the context of the N-YHS chair, they echo the round terminations of the arms, imply the spoils of war, and could be considered as hieroglyphs to be deciphered for messages from the past. P. P. Bober and R. Rubinstein, *Renaissance Artists*

and Antique Sculpture: A Handbook of Sources (New York, 1986), 225–26. In later variant models of the Malmaison *fauteuils*, the sacral plates are replaced by rosettes or leafy foliage along the front seat rail. For a similar eclectic use of trophies, see the design by Pierre-Maximilien Delafontaine commissioned by Napoleon for a mount to frame a large antique agate, the *Grand Camée de la Sainte-Chapelle*, in *Seat of Empire* (CHECKLIST NO. 11).

17. Hall, 342, emblematic of the goddess of Victory.

18. Ibid., 268, notes that roses are symbolic of Venus, goddess of love and fertility. Lewis and Darley, 265, cite their ubiquity in the Neoclassical repertoire. See also ibid., 272–73 (scrolling foliage) and 258–59 (*rinceau*).

19. M. Praz, *On Neoclassicism* (Evanston, Ill., 1969), fig. 24. See also fig. 28, a bronze tripod table from Pompeii whose legs have a foliate ornament similar to those on the stiles of the N-YHS chair.

20. Lewis and Darley, 190, note that with a ring, lion's-head masks were used as handles on ancient Roman furniture and that they are a prominent feature during periods of classical revival.

21. J. D. Draper and C. Le Corbeiller, *The Arts Under Napoleon*, exh. cat. (New York, 1978), n.p., no. 1, and especially E. A. Standen, *European Post-Medieval Tapestries and Related Hangings in the Metropolitan Museum of Art*, vol. 1 (New York, 1986), 419–25. For one version of the Gérard portrait of Bonaparte, set in the throne room of the Tuileries, see B. Chevallier, *Napoleon*, exh. cat., trans. T. M. Gunther (Memphis, 1993), 75, no. 62.

22 W. A. Cooper, *Classical Taste in America 1800–1840*, exh. cat. (New York, 1993), 31–33.

23. G. Tinterow and P. Conisbee, *Portraits by Ingres: Image of an Epoch*, exh. cat. (New York, 1999), 46–49, no. 2, which also illustrates a related drawing in *Seat of Empire* (CHECKLIST NO. 10). The work was commissioned by the First Consul in 1803 and given by him to the city of Liège. See also J. Tulard, A. Fierro, and J.-M. Léri, *L'Histoire de Napoléon par la peinture* (Paris, 1991), 41.

24. Among the other portraits of Bonaparte as First Consul are those painted by Antoine-Jean Gros (1802) and Jean-Baptiste Greuze (1804–05); see Chevallier, *Napoleon*, 62, no. 32; and Y. Cantarel-Bresson, C. Constans, and B. Foucart, *Napoléon: images et histoire. Peintures du château de Versailles (1789–1815)* (Paris, 2001), fig. 222.

25. Only its rear legs, in the shape of balusters, differ. Tulard, Fiero, and Léri, 54, reproduce the drawing, also discussed in J.-P. Samoyault, "Tableaux italiens chosis par Denon pour le Grand Cabinet de l'Em-

pereur aux Tuileries," in A. Avigdor, ed., *Mélanges en hommage à Pierre Rosenberg* (Paris, 2001), 402, no. 9. For the anonymous print after the sheet, see Archives nationales, *Napoléon*, 98–99, no. 433.

26. Similarly Georges Rouget represented Bonaparte—in his painting representing the proclamation of Napoleon as emperor at Saint-Cloud—as standing before a *fauteuil* similar to the N-YHS armchair, whereas Josephine's chair is a *chaise*; see Tulard, Fierro, and Léri, 66. As his imperial ambitions grew, Bonaparte became more obsessed with elaborate protocol.

27. Musée du Louvre, Paris, and Musée national du château, Versailles, *Jacques-Louis David 1748–1825*, exh. cat. (Paris, 1989), 474–77, no. 206.

28. Ibid., 384–86, no. 161; Cantarel-Bresson, Constans, and Foucart, 121–23, fig. 112; and C. Prendergast, *Napoleon and History Painting* (Oxford, 1997), 162–64, fig. 34.

29. Cantarel-Bresson, Constans, and Foucart, fig. 276; and T. Wilson-Smith, *Napoleon and His Artists* (London, 1996), 263.

30. Payne, 89.

31. See, for example, the portraits of Hortense and her son (ca. 1806) seated on an identical but gilded, wider model (*causeuse*) replete with lion's-head mounts (Tulard, Fierro, and Léri, 186); Hortense and her son (ca. 1806–08) standing near a *fauteuil* identical to the one in the artist's portrait of Saint-Jean d'Angély (D. Veron-Denise, "Hortense, Reine de Hollande, et son fils par François Gérard: une acquisition du musée national du château de Fontainebleau," *La Revue du Louvre* 48:1 [1998]: 20–21); Marie-Louise, Napoleon's second wife, and her infant son, the King of Rome (ca. 1811–12), standing before a later gilded variant with lion's–head mounts (Cantarel-Bresson, Constans, and Foucart, fig. 236).

32. According to a letter of 10 May 2001 from Jean-Pierre Samoyault, Joseph Bonaparte also had chairs based on a similar prototype. See Musée national du château de Fontainebleau, *Un ameublement à la mode en 1802: le mobilier du General Moreau*, exh. cat., ed. by J.-P. Samoyault and C. Samoyault Verlet (Paris, 1992), 38–39, no. 30.

33. For a variation by Jacob-Desmalter with a decorative akroterion on its crest rail, see S. O. Haubo, *Kungliga stolar på tio slott*, exh. cat. (Stockholm, 2000), fig. 7.

34. Cooper, 31.

35. The chair (acc. no. 1817.13), made by François Foliot in 1779, was the subject of the special exhibition *Fit for a King* at the New-York Historical Society in 2000, curated by Margaret Hofer.

FIGURE 14

Charles Willson Peale, *Joseph Bonaparte*, 1824 (CHECKLIST NO. 16)

Empire Abroad:

THE FRENCH TASTE IN NEW YORK, 1800–1840

———·———

MARGARET K. HOFER

IN APRIL 1803 President Thomas Jefferson's successful negotiation with Napoleon Bonaparte for the Louisiana Purchase instantly doubled the size of the United States, effectively giving the nation the proportions of a vast empire and positioning it to become a world power. The treaty also signaled the beginnings of a cultural shift, as Americans looked increasingly to Paris, instead of London, for the standards of high style. The triumphal return visit of French hero Marquis de Lafayette to America in 1824, launched with his landing in New York City, provided an additional catalyst for the nation's infatuation with France. During the period from 1800 to 1840, stylish French goods found their way into the homes of many well-to-do urban Americans, but nowhere was the influence of French taste as keenly felt as in New York. Home to growing numbers of prosperous merchants, well-traveled politicians and diplomats, and an influx of European émigrés, New York City embraced the Empire style as a badge of good taste and a symbol of success.

The new French style, exemplified in Napleon's *fauteuil* (armchair), is known today as "Empire" but was referred to as "Grecian," "modern," or "antique" during the period of its reign.[1] Developed by Napoleon's arbiters of taste, designers Charles Percier and Pierre Fontaine, the Empire style was quickly disseminated internationally through a variety of channels. Published pattern books, most notably Percier and Fontaine's *Recueil de décoration intérieures comprenant tout ce qui a rapport à l'ameublement* of 1801, helped spread specific designs and offered a voyeuristic glimpse of interiors actually executed for palaces and aristocratic residences (FIGURE 5). More practical as a guide for cabinetmakers and other craftsmen was Pierre de La Mésangère's *Collection de meubles et objets de goût* ("Collection of Furniture and Objects of Taste"), issued in installments between 1802 and 1835 (CHECKLIST NO. 30). The presence in New York of pattern books such as La Mésangère's is undisputed, as New York craftsmen, including Charles-Honoré Lannuier (1779–1819), modeled furniture after specific Mésangère designs.[2]

While pattern books were an unequivocal source for the transmission of design ideas from Paris to New York, they were only one of many channels of dissemination. New Yorkers traveled abroad in great numbers, seeing firsthand examples of French fashion and purchasing goods for shipment back to the United States. French émigrés, particularly those exiled by Napoleon, or Napoleon's supporters banished from France after his fall from power, flocked to New York for its vibrant émigré community, bringing with them art, furnishings, and a variety of decorative goods expressing the latest in French taste. Among these early nineteenth-century expatriates were a number of skilled craftsmen who imported their direct working knowledge of the Empire style. French goods also flowed into New York City to fill the shops of fancy goods retailers, where they were sold alongside domestic manufactures and merchandise from England.

"All the world is going to Europe," remarked New York diarist Philip Hone, who served as New York's mayor in 1825.[3] While the tradition of gentlemen touring Europe for education and enlightenment extended back to the eighteenth century, new incentives lured increasing numbers of male and female American visitors abroad in the early years of the nineteenth century. The period from 1815 to 1830 witnessed a surge in the numbers of Americans traveling to France. The cessation of the Napoleonic Wars had made European travel attractive again, and huge numbers of Americans sailed across the Atlantic in search of cultural refinement, as well as a firsthand glimpse of the latest French fashions.[4] New York City experienced meteoric growth in the 1820s, becoming the nation's preeminent seaport, emporium, and financial center.[5] Commercial success fed cultural ambition, and the city's upwardly mobile population was drawn to Europe, particularly to Paris, for exposure to the artistic amenities and French-made material goods that were synonymous with Continental sophistication.

The tradition of New Yorkers traveling abroad and falling under the spell of French art and culture originated in the eighteenth century. United States minister to France Gouverneur Morris, in Paris from 1788 to 1794, developed a connoisseur's passion for French decorative arts. Morris made shrewd purchases of stylish objects for himself, President George Washington, and other American friends. After his return to New York, Morris displayed his French treasures at Morrisania, his manor house in what later became the Bronx. Here many New Yorkers received their first glimpse of high-style French furnishings, including some pieces directly from the palace of Versailles.[6] Robert R. Livingston, another great Francophile, served as minister to France from 1801 to 1804 and spent an additional year traveling through Europe with his family. Livingston acquired numerous French furnishings for his Hudson River estate, Clermont, including silver, furniture, porcelain, and metalwork.[7] While in Paris, Livingston met the young American inventor, Robert Fulton, his eventual partner in developing the first successful steamboat on the Hudson River. Fulton married his partner's second cousin Harriet Livingston in 1808, and the new couple was presented with a stylish French dressing table as a wedding gift from Robert Livingston. Imported from France, this table would have adorned Fulton's fine New York City town house at the corner of Marketfield and State, suggesting a cultural sophistication on a par with his technological and commercial success.[8]

Perhaps the most significant diplomatic couple to travel in France was James Monroe and his beautiful wife, Elizabeth Kortright Monroe, daughter of a prominent New York merchant. While in Paris from 1794 to 1796 and again from 1803 to 1807, the Monroes acquired a passion for French taste that they carried back to the United States, and eventually transported to the White House.[9] They returned with numerous French purchases, including a set of armchairs derived from designs of Percier and Fontaine.[10] More important, they continued to order goods from Paris as residents of the White House, setting a national trend for appreciation of French style. In 1817 the Monroes ordered a suite of carved and gilded furniture by Parisian cabinetmaker Pierre-Antoine Bellangé (CHECKLIST NO. 5). President Monroe ran some political risk by ordering from France, because public sentiment favored the support of domestic manufacturers. The President felt strongly, however, that the Bellangé furniture, some of which is still displayed in the Blue Room of the White House, suited the dignity and character of the nation.[11]

Although diplomats may have been among the most passionate Francophiles, New York merchants expressed a strong attachment to French style through their purchasing power. William Bayard, one of New York City's wealthiest and most notable citizens, ordered French-made goods from Paris, had his children schooled at home with French tutors, and sent at least one of his sons to school in Paris.[12] When his daughters Harriet and Maria both married in 1817, he provided each with a dowry that included furniture by French-trained New York cabinetmaker Charles-Honoré Lannuier and a suite of seating furniture from Paris (CHECKLIST NO. 6).[13] The suite received by Maria is described in detail in a surviving invoice, which mentions "sixteen chairs in mahogany, with square backs, carved legs, and gilded brass mounts, two upholstered armchairs and one sofa in mahogany, with carved legs and gilded-brass mounts."[14] The French suite would have held pride of place in Maria and Duncan Campbell's elegantly appointed house at 51 Broadway, whose front parlor included a Lannuier-made pier table with gilded swan supports surmounted by a six-foot-tall gilded French pier glass, no doubt completed by a window treatment in the latest French style.[15] The Campbell mansion, outfitted by and for the newlyweds in 1817, very likely represented the height of contemporary fashion in New York. Reflecting the wealth and influence of Maria's father, William Bayard, the home also demonstrated the taste of a young couple honed by first-hand European experience. In 1814–15, Maria Bayard traveled to England and France, taking close note of the latest French styles, remarking on dress and furnishings, and even catching sight of Emperor Napoleon.[16]

New York City's welcoming attitude toward political exiles, combined with its reputation for religious, political, and cultural tolerance, made it a haven for French émigrés during the late-eighteenth and early nineteenth centuries. The size of New York City's French-born population was never large, particularly when compared to the city's swelling numbers of Irish and German immigrants. In fact, the New York Census of 1845 (the first to record place of birth) cited only 3,710 French-born residents, comprising one percent of the city's total population.[17] Throughout the period from 1800 to 1840, French émigrés, predominantly Catholic, worshipped at the ethnically mixed St. Peter's Church on Barclay Street, where sermons were preached in multiple languages. New York's French Catholics did not establish their own parish until 1840, when the Church of St. Vincent de Paul was organized by Comte de Forbin-Janson, Bishop of Nancy, France. The church erected its first building in 1842 on Canal Street between Broadway and Lafayette Streets, and moved to West 23rd Street in 1858.[18] The fact that so few organizations—social, religious, artistic, and business—were established by and specifically for the French community suggests that this group assimilated with relative ease into the cultural fabric of New York City. The generally high economic and social status of French émigrés in the city during the first half of the nineteenth century also facilitated their acceptance by native New Yorkers, particularly because to fashionable society the French elite epitomized good taste and sophistication. In a city gripped by "Gallomania," it is not surprising that French immigrants and visitors received a warm welcome.[19]

Many French émigrés passed through the city with little notice, but a few left indelible marks on New York City's cultural life. The French general Jean-Victor-Marie Moreau, the prominent commander of Napoleon's army arrested in 1804 for plotting against him, spent several years of his exile in America, keeping an estate in Morrisville, Pennsylvania, and a house in New York City. From 1809 to 1813,

General Moreau and his wife, Louise-Alexandrine-Eugénie Hulot, maintained a residence at 119 Pearl Street.[20] The Moreaus may well have tried to recreate in New York the stylistic sensibility of their *hôtel* in the rue d'Anjou in Paris, which had been renovated and decorated in 1801 by none other than Percier and Fontaine. Engravings of designs for the Moreau home reproduced in the *Recueil* (plates 19 and 60) demonstrate some of the same stylistic features of Napoleon's *fauteuil*, particularly Madame Moreau's bed, executed by Jacob Frères in 1802. Although none of the furnishings associated with the Moreaus during their American exile have come to light, one must assume that Madame Moreau, a leader of French society in New York, would have purchased only the finest and most up-to-date of French fashions.[21] By 1811 she had established ties with Lannuier, New York's leading cabinetmaker in the French style, loaning him $2,000 and holding a mortgage on his property as collateral.[22] Although no specific furniture transactions have been identified, it can be assumed that Madame Moreau provided assistance in the form of patronage as well as cash.

When General Moreau was killed in battle shortly after returning to Europe in 1813, the contents of the couple's Pearl Street town house were sold at auction. An announcement in the *Mercantile Advertiser* itemized the elegant furnishings to be auctioned, including "large Pier Looking Glasses, several large Chandeliers, Pier Tables, Mahogany Dinning [*sic*], Tea and Card Tables, Mahogany Sophas [*sic*] and Chairs, Gilt Chairs with fancy Satin Cushions, . . . Mahogany Bed Steads . . . several handsome sets of Window Curtains, a Grand Piano forte . . . various sets of elegant French China."[23] Undoubtedly many of these items, vetted with the tacit endorsement of one of New York's ultimate arbiters of French taste, found their way into fashion-conscious New York homes, further solidifying the vogue for French Empire style on this side of the Atlantic.

A year after the public sale of the Moreaus' furnishings, a new arrival brought a further wave of French influence across the ocean. Joseph Bonaparte, the elder brother of Napoleon (whose ownership of the *fauteuil* is outlined in the preceding catalogue essay "From Paris to Point Breeze: The History of Napoleon's Armchair in France and America") disembarked in New York City, eventually settling in Bordentown, New Jersey, 65 miles south of the city. He maintained firm social and political connections with New York throughout the duration of his American sojourns (1815–32, 1835–36, 1838–39), and he deeply influenced cultural life there. Surviving correspondence written by Joseph Bonaparte to friends in New York, including Madame Stephen Jumel and Chancellor Robert R. Livingston, confirm active social ties that encouraged the emperor's brother to make frequent visits to New York.[24] He wrote his friend Livingston in 1820, "I always have plans to spend part of the winter in New York, but at intervals, in order to see my friends there."[25] Poet Fitz-Greene Halleck was present at a wedding party in New York City for a member of Joseph Bonaparte's entourage, attended by many French émigrés including several old heroes of Waterloo. Joseph was observed blowing a paper trumpet; Marshal Grouchy, singing military songs; and General Lallemand, crawling around playing horse for a little boy.[26] In many respects, it would appear that Joseph Bonaparte felt quite at home in his adopted country.

In addition to spending time in the city, Bonaparte owned extensive land holdings in upstate New York, in company with other French émigrés. In the summer of 1818 Bonaparte made his first journey to the Black River area of northern New York State (near present-day Watertown), to view the lands he had purchased three years earlier from French land speculator

FIGURE 15

French maker, Pier table from Point
Breeze, ca. 1801–15, Philadelphia
Museum of Art (1950-49-1)

James Leray de Chaumont.[27] Leray intended to develop his vast tracts of land in northern New York, some owned jointly with Gouverneur Morris, into a colony for French émigrés, but never fully realized his objective. However, Joseph Bonaparte was delighted with the 26,840 acres of wilderness, and he eventually built three houses and a hunting lodge on his property.[28] During the summer months (long, cold winters made off-season travel nearly impossible) Bonaparte entertained a growing population of French émigrés at Natural Bridge and on Lake Diana (later renamed Lake Bonaparte), and organized elaborate hunting parties and moonlit musicales. Among the visitors to Leray's and Bonaparte's northern wilderness were Governor DeWitt Clinton and President James Monroe.[29]

While in America, Joseph Bonaparte worked tirelessly on the political front advocating the restoration of Napoleon, and later Napoleon II, to the throne of France. He chose New York City as the locus of his

activity, and in 1828 established the French-language newspaper *Le Courrier des États-Unis* there (FIGURE 8). Subtitled "Journal Politique et Littéraire," the newspaper survived well into the twentieth century. Bonaparte entrusted the paper's management to Félix Lacoste. Intended more for readers in France than in New York (packet boats carried large numbers of copies across the ocean), the *Courrier* provided a voice for the large population of Bonapartists in the northeastern United States.[30]

Joseph Bonaparte's influence on the artistic and cultural life of New York had even more significant and lasting impact than his political activity. He was widely admired for his generous patronage of the arts in New York and Philadelphia. He attended the first performance of an opera by an Italian company in New York City in 1825 and the first ballet performed by a French company he had helped sponsor.[31] Bonaparte's vast art collection, composed of more than two hundred European paintings and dozens of busts and statues, amazed American visitors. A few troubled guests commented on the meager clothing worn by the young women depicted in some of Joseph Bonaparte's paintings.[32] Visitors also observed elaborate furnishings in the Empire style, much of it mahogany with gilt metal mounts.[33] Surviving examples of Point Breeze furniture include a pair of French mahogany pier tables made about 1800–10, with numerous ormolu mounts, a black marble top, and Egyptian figural supports (FIGURE 15).[34] The riches of Bonaparte's collections of fine and decorative arts were dispersed to an inquisitive and enthusiastic audience at a major auction of the contents of Point Breeze in 1847.[35] Organized by New York auctioneer Anthony J. Bleecker, the sale took place at the estate on 25 June 1847, attracting friends, neighbors, and collectors eager for a souvenir of the late ex-king. Many objects with a history of purchase at the 1847 sale (some better substantiated than others) survive today in museum and private collections (FIGURES 14 AND 15).

Joseph Bonaparte patronized American portrait and landscape painters, whose surviving canvases provide revealing glimpses of the royal expatriate in his adopted country. His character is astutely rendered in the 1824 likeness painted by Charles Willson Peale (FIGURE 14), which captures features noted in 1816 by Philadelphian Harriet Manigault, who described Bonaparte as "short & fat," with "a most good-natured countenance," and looking "more like a farmer than a *King*."[36] Another American visitor to Point Breeze decided that Joseph "had to my eye little or none of a foreign physiognomy—his person of good size, of neat & genteel form, & on the whole, such as we often see in a pretty Gentleman—his head was of good proportion—his profile feature regular—a neat mouth & teeth—blue eyes & rather fair complexion . . . the King appeared to be a man of soft manners . . . moderate temper, & very free from arrogance & pride."[37]

The character of Bonaparte's Point Breeze estate was also captured in oil on canvas. Local artist Charles B. Lawrence painted numerous views that evoke the idyllic landscape that Bonaparte had painstakingly created. The Lawrence painting *View from Bordentown Hill on the Delaware (Point Breeze)* (FIGURE 7), once owned by Bonaparte's personal secretary Louis Mailliard, shows the second, grander mansion that Joseph built after his first house was destroyed by fire in 1820.[38] In the foreground Lawrence depicts the park-like setting laid out by Bonaparte to resemble the grounds of the Escorial, the sixteenth-century Spanish palace. The estate included twelve miles of carriage roads winding through groves of trees and over stone bridges; rustic gazebos to provide shelter from the rain; and verdant knolls ornamented with statuary. Joseph formed the scenic body of water seen on the right side of the painting by damming Crosswicks Creek, a tributary of the Delaware River. This picturesque lake became the perfect site for his European swans and swan-shaped pleasure boats.[39]

Joseph Bonaparte amassed one of the finest collections of fine and decorative arts in this country, and probably provided many Americans with their first real glimpse of old master paintings. He was an active member of the Pennsylvania Academy of the Fine Arts, in Philadelphia, frequently lending works of art for exhibition, including a portrait of his brother Napoleon and paintings by David, Vernet, and Rubens.[40] The great double portrait of Joseph's daughters, Charlotte and Zénaïde, painted by Jacques-Louis David in 1821 and featuring a carved and gilded sofa related to Napoleon's *fauteuil*, was loaned to the Pennsylvania Academy in 1823 and subsequently hung at Point Breeze.[41] His daughter Charlotte, a painter in her own right who studied with David in Paris, exhibited her work at the Academy. Joseph Bonaparte's activities in the artistic sphere of New York City are less well documented. However, it is interesting to note that Joseph and Napoleon Bonaparte were honorary members of the New York Academy of Arts, established in 1802 by Mayor Edward Livingston of New York and his brother, U.S. Minster to France Robert R. Livingston. In 1804 the new emperor gave the organization a complete set of twenty-four volumes of engravings by the eighteenth-century Italian master Giovanni Battista Piranesi, which the Academy's founders hoped would provide inspiration to New York's young painters, sculptors, and others "occupied in works of taste."[42]

Numerous craftsmen in early nineteenth-century New York were indeed busy creating "works of taste." Discouraged by fierce competition and an uncertain future in France, an influx of French émigré craftsmen and specialists in other trades sought a fresh start and economic opportunities in New York City. Along with the skills of their trade, these émigrés carried firsthand knowledge of French design, helped to spread the Empire style, and as a result influenced New Yorkers' embrace of the French taste. The best example of such a craftsman is Charles-Honoré Lannuier, whose appearance on the scene in 1803 gave new impetus to the furniture trade in New York.[43] Lannuier announced his arrival in a newspaper advertisement, describing himself as "just arrived from France," having "worked at his trade with the most celebrated Cabinet Makers of Europe." He made special note of his ability to make furniture "in the newest and latest French fashion" and the availability of his stock of "new patterns."[44] Lannuier also traded on his French origins in the labels he affixed to his furniture. Two of the three labels Lannuier applied to his New York-made furniture were bilingual, a nod to his émigré clientele and a reminder of his chic French lineage.[45]

Lannuier soon became a leading rival of the well-established New York cabinetmaker Duncan Phyfe (1768—1854), whose furniture adhered more to Eng-

FIGURE 16

Charles-Honoré Lannuier,
Card table from Point Breeze, 1810—15 (CHECKLIST NO. 3)

lish Regency designs. Lannuier's melding of pure French style tempered with elements of New York's favored Regency style indicates that he was influenced by the furniture of New York craftsmen and responsive to the stylistic preferences of his clientele. Lannuier's early New York work (pre-1812) displays more of the local vernacular than his later work (1812-19) in the full-blown French style.[46] The card table with a history of ownership by Joseph Bonaparte (FIGURE 16), made about 1810-15, manifests this marriage of French and English style.[47] The crisp profile of the top, the Egyptian-inspired inlay across the apron, and the Tuscan-style support columns, all relate to French Empire taste. The English-style base, with its four reeded and water leaf carved legs and claw feet, is in the standard Phyfe style.[48] Unlike the Point Breeze card table,

FIGURE 17

Charles-Honoré Lannuier, French press, 1812–19 (CHECKLIST NO. 4)

inscribed with Lannuier's name. Recent analysis of the finish layers revealed that it was originally patinated to resemble antique bronze, much like the *bronzé* finish on the Napoleon *fauteuil.*[49]

Ample evidence indicates that Lannuier and his French-style furniture found wide acceptance in New York and beyond. In 1812 Lannuier received an important commission from the city to provide armchairs for City Hall, newly completed after designs of John McComb, Jr. and Joseph François Mangin. The most important public structure in the city at the time, the building was itself a blend of English and French Neoclassical styles. Lannuier provided a set of twenty-four mahogany upholstered-back armchairs for the Common Council Chamber, perfectly suited to the designs of the room. The overall form of the armchairs is based on French types, and some of the decorative elements, such as the inlaid stars, reflect Napoleonic influence. The treatment of the water leaf-carved arm supports and swelled reeded legs, however, is clearly derived from English Regency design.[50]

Like their furniture-making counterparts, French artisans in other trades made their way to New York to take advantage of the strengthening market for French goods. New York entrepreneur Dr. Henry Mead attempted the manufacture of porcelain in New York in 1819 by luring "some first rate workmen imported from France" and setting up a porcelain factory to produce wares "equal in firmness to the French."[51] Mead's short-lived endeavor (he ceased operation by 1825) was soon followed by the arrival of French partners Louis François Decasse and Nicolas Louis Edouard Chanou, who established a porcelain manufactory on the same site. A former apprentice at the Sèvres factory in France, Chanou brought to the partnership technical expertise in the manufacture of porcelain. Decasse and Chanou's business was cut short by a disastrous fire in 1827, and few examples of

Lannuier's French press (FIGURE 17), made for New York hardware merchant Garret Byvanck Abeel about 1812–19, is considered a pure French form. Specifically mentioned in the New York cabinetmaker's price book of 1810, the "French press" (a large clothing cupboard with two paneled doors) had entered the vocabulary of New York artisans. The pediment of the Abeel press bears a cast-plaster bust of a Roman figure

their work survive. An extant tea service by Decasse and Chanou, however, provides telling information about their products. Although the porcelain body directly imitates French hard-paste porcelain, the forms of the tea vessels are distinctly English in design.[52] Like Lannuier, Decasse and Chanou responded to the New York market by providing goods they knew would find a receptive audience.

During the period from 1800 to 1840, upper- and middle-class New Yorkers were beguiled by the seductive power of French taste: its classical references, heroic overtones, and aura of sophistication. British traveler Frances Trollope acidly observed New Yorkers' weakness for French fashion during her visit there in 1827, "If it were not for the peculiar manner of walking which distinguishes all American women, Broadway might be taken for a French street, where it was the fashion for very smart ladies to promenade. The dress is entirely French; not an article . . . must be English, on pain of being stigmatized as out of the fashion. Everything English is decidedly *mauvais ton*."[53] Ladies' fashion on the street closely paralleled the furnishings of parlors within the "smart" homes lining lower Broadway. But clearly, as the products of Lannuier, Decasse and Chanou, and others indicate, New Yorkers did not entirely abandon a predilection for more restrained English design. Ultimately New York craftsmen and consumers together forged a distinctive hybrid expression incorporating the French Empire style, transmitted via design books, émigré visitors and their furnishings, and the products of émigré craftsmen. It is ironic that Napoleon's armchair, a powerful symbol of a European empire, ended up in America, a country driven by democratic ideals. On the other hand, it is entirely appropriate that the *fauteuil*, a pioneering example of Empire design, should make its final home in a city once captivated and transformed by the Empire style.

1. W. A. Cooper, *Classical Taste in America 1800–1840*, exh. cat. (New York, 1993), 10.
2. For example, Lannuier adapted La Mésangère designs for the crown of a bedstead made for Mrs. Isaac Bell about 1812–19 (Bartow-Pell Mansion Museum, Bronx), and for a pair of pier tables purchased by French émigré James Leray de Chaumont about 1815–19 (private collection).
3. F. R. Dulles, *Americans Abroad: Two Centuries of European Travel* (Ann Arbor, 1964), 1.
4. Cooper, 26–27.
5. E. G. Burrows and M. Wallace, *Gotham: A History of New York City to 1898* (New York, 1999), 450.
6. L. Schreider III, "Gouverneur Morris: Connoisseur of French Art," *Apollo* 93:111 (1971): 481–82. Gouverneur Morris attended the Versailles auctions of 1793–94, purchasing several pieces of furniture from Marie Antoinette's *cabinet intérieur de la reine*. Among his acquisitions was a side chair (*chaise*) made by François Foliot in 1779 specifically to seat the king. The *chaise* was donated to the New-York Historical Society by Gouverneur Morris's widow in 1817 (acc. no. 1817.13) and was the subject of the exhibition *Fit for a King*, presented by the New-York Historical Society in 2000.
7. Cooper, 33–34. Livingston purchased French goods in the latest taste as well as secondhand items at auction. The New-York Historical Society has a silver coffeepot (acc. no. 1951.284) made by silversmith Jacques-Nicolas Roettiers in 1775 that was likely acquired by Livingston while he was in Paris and subsequently engraved with his coat of arms.
8. Ibid., 34; and Burrows and Wallace, 343. The dressing table is owned by Clermont State Historic Site, Germantown, New York.
9. Cooper, 29.
10. Ibid. The chairs are at the James Monroe Museum, Fredericksburg, Virginia.
11. C. E. Conger and B. C. Monkman, "President Monroe's Acquisitions," *Connoisseur* 192:771 (1976): 56–63.
12. P. M. Kenny et al., *Honoré Lannuier, Cabinetmaker from Paris*, exh. cat. (New York, 1998), 105–06. The Bayard-Campbell-Pearsall Papers at the New York Public Library and the William Bayard Papers in the Library of the New-York Historical Society provide extensive evidence of Bayard's French patronage.
13. Ibid., 110. Harriet Bayard married Stephen Van Rensselaer IV of Albany, and Maria Bayard married Duncan Pearsall Campbell.
14. Ibid., 113–14. The original invoice, in French, is at the New York Public Library in the Bayard-Campbell-Pearsall Papers.
15. Ibid., 114.
16. Ibid., 111. Maria Bayard's diary from her trip abroad is in the Bayard-Campbell-Pearsall papers at the New York Public Library.

17. I. Rosenwaike, *Population History of New York City* (Syracuse, 1972), 42. The same census counted 96,581 Irish and 24,416 German immigrants.

18. H. Binsse, "The Church of Saint Vincent de Paul (The French Church), New York" *Historical Records and Studies* 12 (1918): 102–13. Félix Lacoste's funeral in November 1853 was held at Saint Vincent de Paul, often referred to as the "French Church."

19. Burrows and Wallace, 322–23.

20. Kenny et al., 130.

21. Ibid., 131.

22. Ibid.

23. "Sale of Furniture...the Household Furniture of the late Gen. Moreau," *Mercantile Advertiser*, 2 March 1814.

24. Joseph Bonaparte to Mrs. Stephen Jumel, 9 April 1819, the New-York Historical Society; and Joseph Bonaparte to Robert R. Livingston, 1 November 1820 and 15 January 1832, Robert R. Livingston Papers, the New-York Historical Society.

25. Bonaparte to Livingston, 1 November 1820. The original French reads, "J'ai toujours le projet de passer une partie de l'hiver à New York, mais par intervalles, pour y voir mes amis."

26. O. Connelly, *The Gentle Bonaparte: A Biography of Joseph, Napoleon's Elder Brother* (New York, 1968), 270. Halleck's observations are recorded in J. G. Wilson, *Life and Letters of Fitz-Greene Halleck* (New York, 1869).

27. T. W. Clarke, *Émigrés in the Wilderness* (New York, 1941), 127, 133.

28. Ibid., 133.

29. Kenny et al., 130.

30. G. Girod de L'Ain, *Joseph Bonaparte, Le Roi Malgré Lui* (Paris, 1970), 393–94.

31. Connelly, 270.

32. E. M. Woodward, *Bonaparte's Park and the Murats* (Trenton, N.J., 1879), 53. One visitor to Point Breeze commented: "The walls were covered with oil paintings, particularly of young females, with less clothing about them than they or you would have found comfortable in our cold climate, and much less than we found agreeable."

33. Girod de L'Ain, 350.

34. Cooper, 71. The tables were purchased at the 1847 auction of Bonaparte's estate by his close friend, Philadelphian Joseph Hopkinson.

35. A. J. Bleecker, *Catalogue of Rare, Original Paintings...Valuable Engravings, Elegant Sculpture, Household Furniture...Belonging to the Late Joesph Napoleon Bonaparte...to be sold...on Friday, June 25, 1847* (New York, 1847). An earlier auction in 1845 dispersed the contents of Joseph Bonaparte's library.

36. H. Manigault, *Diary of Harriet Manigault, 1813–1816*, ed. V. and J. S. Armentrout (Rockland, Maine, 1976), 132–33.

37. J. F. Watson, "Trip to Pennsbury & to Count Survilliers—1826," unpublished mss., the Winterthur Library.

38. C. B. Bradley, "Point Breeze and the Mailliards," *Proceedings of the New Jersey Historical Society* 78:2 (1960): 75–81. Louis Mailliard, reportedly one of several illegitimate children of Joseph Bonaparte, was named executor of his estate. The Lawrence painting is not specifically listed in Bonaparte's will and may have been, like the *fauteuil*, a gift made to a close associate before returning to Europe in 1839.

39. Woodward, 42–43; and P. T. Stroud, *The Emperor of Nature: Charles-Lucien Bonaparte and His World* (Philadelphia, 2000), 37–38.

40. B. B. Garvan, *Federal Philadelphia 1785–1825* (Philadelphia, 1987), 80.

41. Ibid. The David portrait, illustrated on p. 61, is now at the J. Paul Getty Museum. See also Musée du Louvre, Paris, and Musée national du château, Versailles, *Jacques-Louis David 1748–1825*, exh. cat. (Paris, 1989), 530–32, no. 231.

42. Cooper, 79–80.

43. Other examples of French émigré cabinetmakers in New York, all employed in Lannuier's shop, include his first cousin Jean-Charles Cochois, François Chailleau, Pierre-Aurore Frichot, and Jean Gruez. See Kenny et al., 49–52.

44. *New-York Evening Post*, 15 July 1803.

45. Lannuier's labels and *estampille* are discussed in Kenny et al., 149–54. Lannuier's third label incorporates several misspellings of English words, perhaps deliberately: "Hre Lannuier, Cabinet Maker from Paris Kips is Whare house of new fashion fourniture Broad Street, No 60, New-York. Hre Lannuier, Ebéniste de Paris, Tient Fabrique & Magasin de Meubles les plus à la Mode, New-York."

46. Ibid., 76. Peter Kenny originally noted the combination of French and "New York vernacular" styles in a nearly identical labeled Lannuier card table.

47. According to a notarized note found with the table's mate, the pair of tables was purchased at the 1847 sale of Bonaparte's estate by John Stokes Bryan and General William T. Rogers of Doylestown, Pennsylvania. The Bonaparte provenance is inconclusive: lot 91 of the 1847 catalogue lists "Two mahogany Lyre front card tables," which could be the Lannuier pair. However, "lyre front" could also refer to a table with a lyre support rather than a small inlaid lyre. If the card tables did in fact come from Point Breeze, they must have been purchased by Bonaparte secondhand, since their manufacture predates his arrival in the U.S. See ibid., 207; and E. Feld and S. P. Feld, *Of the Newest Fashion*, exh. cat. (New York, 2001), 29.

48. Kenny et al., 76. Kenny also notes that the table's Tuscan-style columns bear a striking similarity to the arm supports on a French *fauteuil* made by Jacob Frères for General Moreau about 1800.

49. Ibid., 84–85.

50. Ibid., 140–43 and 201. Twenty-two of Lannuier's armchairs remain at City Hall.

51. *New York Commercial Advertiser*, 7 October 1819; and *Niles Weekly Register*, 27 February 1819, as quoted in A. C. Frelinghuysen, *American Porcelain 1770–1920* (New York, 1989), 11–12.

52. Frelinghuysen, 80.

53. F. Trollope, *Domestic Manners of the Americans* (London, 1832), 179.

CHECKLIST OF THE EXHIBITION

FURNITURE

1. Jacob Frères (French, active 1797–1803)
   Armchair (*fauteuil*), 1800
   Painted and gilded beech; original under-upholstery and red wool showcover; silk, velvet, and gilded silver trim
   38 x 26 x 28 in. (96.5 x 68 x 71 cm)
   The New-York Historical Society, Gift of Louis Borg, 1867.438
   (FIGURES 1, 9, 13, 18)

   From the Salle du Conseil, Malmaison

2. Jacob Frères (French, active 1797–1803)
   Stool (*tabouret*), 1800
   Painted and gilded beech; replacement showcover
   30 x 28 13/16 x 18 13/16 in. (72 x 75 x 47 cm)
   Stamped: *JACOB FRERES / RUE MESLEE*
   Musée national du château de Malmaison, MM.54.9.1
   (FIGURE 12)

   From the Salle du Conseil, Malmaison

3. Charles-Honoré Lannuier (French, 1779–1819, active in New York City 1803–19)
   Card table, 1810–15
   Mahogany; mahogany veneer, white pine, yellow poplar; brass inlay and mounts; baize
   30 7/8 x 36 5/8 x 18 3/8 in. (78.5 x 93 x 46.75 cm) closed
   Private Collection, New York
   (FIGURE 16)

   Reportedly purchased at the 1847 auction of the contents of Joseph Bonaparte's estate, Point Breeze

4. Charles-Honoré Lannuier (French, 1779–1819, active in New York City 1803–19)
   French press, 1812–19
   Mahogany; mahogany veneer, yellow poplar, white pine, brass, plaster
   101 3/4 x 63 x 25 3/4 in. (258.4 x 160 x 65.4 cm)
   Inscribed on underside of plaster bust:
   H. Lannuier / New York
   The New-York Historical Society, Gift of Mrs. William Hyde Wheeler, 1943.368
   (FIGURE 17)

   Owned by New York merchant Garret Byvanck Abeel

5. Pierre-Antoine Bellangé (French, 1758–1827)
   Armchair (*fauteuil*), 1817
   Gilded beech; replacement showcover
   38 1/2 x 25 1/2 x 22 in. (47.8 x 64.8 x 55.9 cm)
   Woodrow Wilson House, National Trust Historic Site, Washington, D.C., on extended loan to the Baltimore Museum of Art, R.14199

   Ordered by President James Monroe for the White House in 1817

6. French maker
   Side chair (*chaise*), 1817
   Mahogany, gilded brass; replacement showcover
   36 x 19 x 15 in. (91.5 x 48.3 x 40 cm)
   The Albany Institute of History and Art, New York, Gift of Stephen Van Rensselaer Crosby, 1957

   Wedding gift to Maria Bayard and Duncan Pearsall Campbell (married 1817) of New York City

PAINTINGS, DRAWINGS, AND WATERCOLORS

7. Charles Percier (French, 1764–1838)
   Album of architectural and decorative drawings, open to folio 19r, ca. 1800–15
   Six in graphite, one in pen and black ink over graphite on various papers mounted on a larger sheet in a parchment-covered album from the stationer Renault
   14 1/2 x 9 1/2 in. (36.7 x 24.3 cm)
   The Metropolitan Museum of Art, New York, The Elisha Whittelsey Collection, The Elisha Whittelsey Fund, 63.535

8. Attributed to François-Pascal-Simon Baron Gérard (French, 1770–1837)
   The Signing of the Concordat between France and the Papacy on 16 July 1801, ca. 1801
   Black chalk, pen and black ink with white heightening on paper
   18 7/8 x 23 5/8 in. (48 x 60 cm)
   Musée national des châteaux de Versailles et de Trianon, Versailles, MV. 2572 Inv. Dessins 920

9. French artist
   View of the Château of Malmaison from the Park, ca. 1802–05
   Gouache and graphite on paper
   9 1/2 x 13 5/8 in. (23.7 x 34 cm)
   Musée national du château de Malmaison, MM. 99.11.1

10. Jean-Auguste-Dominique Ingres (French, 1780–1867)
    Study for "*Bonaparte as First Consul*," ca. 1803–04
    Pen and brown ink with wash on paper
    8 7/8 x 6 in. (22.5 x 15.2 cm)
    Private Collection

11. Pierre-Maximilien Delafontaine
(French, 1777–1860)
Design for the mount for a large antique
agate in the Cabinet Nationale (*Grand
Camée de la Sainte-Chapelle*), 1807
Pen and brown and red ink, and brown wash
over graphite on paper, with several smaller
pieces mounted on the primary sheet
30 x 21 3/4 in. (76.2 x 55.2 cm)
Signed and dated at lower middle: *PM. Delafontaine 1807*; inscribed at lower right: *mon-
ture de l'agatte du Cabinet national[e]*
Private Collection, New York

Commissioned by Napoleon Bonaparte

12. François-Pascal-Simon Baron Gérard
(French, 1770–1837)
*Michel, Count Regnaud
de Saint-Jean d'Angély*, 1808
Oil on canvas
85 1/2 x 56 in. (217 x 142 cm)
Musée national des châteaux de Versailles
et de Trianon, Versailles, M.V. 5753

13. Jean-Victor Nicolle (French, 1754–1826)
*View of the Cour d'honneur of the
Château of Malmaison*, ca. 1810
Watercolor, pen and black ink, and graphite
on paper
8 1/8 x 12 15/16 in. (20.5 x 32.3 cm)
Musée national du château de Malmaison,
MM.2000.27.1
(FIGURE 4)

14. Charles B. Lawrence
(American, ca. 1790–1837)
*View from Bordentown Hill on the Delaware
(Point Breeze)*, ca. 1820–30
Oil on canvas
37 1/2 x 45 1/2 in. (95.3 x 115.5 cm)
New Jersey Historical Society, Newark, New
Jersey, Gift of Mrs. J. W. Mailliard, 1957.62
(FIGURE 7)

15. Emile-Jean-Horace Vernet
(French, 1789–1863)
*Napoleon Meditating on a
Military Map at Charleroi*, 1823
Oil on canvas
13 x 15 13/16 in. (33 x 40 cm)
The New-York Historical Society, Gift of
Thomas Jefferson Bryan, 1867.268

16. Charles Willson Peale
(American, 1741–1827)
Joseph Bonaparte, 1824
Oil on canvas
30 x 24 in. (76.2 x 61 cm)
Historical Society of Pennsylvania,
Philadelphia, Pennsylvania, 3.1896
(FIGURE 14)

OTHER DECORATIVE ARTS

17. Pierre Louis Dagoty (French, 1771–1840)
Dessert plate, 1800–10
Porcelain, overglaze enamel decoration,
and gilding (etched)
8 3/8 in. (21.2 cm) diameter
One other plate in the set of 12 signed on the
reverse: *Dagoty A PAris*
Private Collection, New York

18. Bartolomeo Franzoni (Italian, 18th–early
19th century), after Antoine-Denis Chaudet
(French, 1763–1810)
Napoleon, 1807–10
Marble (Carrara)
23 1/2 in. (59.7 cm) height
The Metropolitan Museum of Art, New
York, lent by Maximilian E. Sands, OL.153.1

19. Gobelins, Workshop of Michel-Henri
Cozette (French, 1744–1822), after
François-Pascal-Simon Baron Gérard
Weavers: Harland, Abel-Nicolas Sollier,
Duruy *fils*, et al.
Tapestry: *Napoleon I in His Coronation Robes*,
1808–11
Wool, silk, and gilded silver thread in
original gilded pine frame
87 1/2 x 57 1/2 in. (222 x 146 cm)
The Metropolitan Museum of Art, New
York, Purchase, Joseph Pulitzer Bequest,
1943 (43.99)
(FIGURE 11)

20. English maker (Staffordshire)
Pitcher, 1814–20
White earthenware, with transfer printed
and overglaze enamel decoration
6 5/8 x 7 x 5 in. (16.8 x 17.8 x 12.7 cm)
Inscribed on front: *BONNY in his NEW
CLOTHES*, with additional text
The New-York Historical Society, Gift of
Miss Jean Morron and Mr. and Mrs. L. R.
Burch in memory of John R. Morron and
Belle G. Morron, 1951.136

21. English maker (Staffordshire)
Pitcher, 1814–20
White earthenware, with transfer printed
and overglaze enamel decoration
6 7/8 x 6 7/8 x 5 in. (17.5 x 17.5 x 14.5 cm)
Printed on neck: *BONAPARTE DETHRON'D
APRIL 1st 1814*, with additional text
The New-York Historical Society, Gift of
Miss Jean Morron and Mr. and Mrs. L. R.
Burch in memory of John R. Morron and
Belle G. Morron, 1951.130

22. Unknown maker
Napoleon Bonaparte, early 19th century
Ivory
1 7/8 x 1 x 1/2 in. (4.8 x 2.5 x 1.3 cm)
The New-York Historical Society, Gift of
Thomas Jefferson Bryan, 1867.383

23. French maker
Mantel clock: *The Chariot of Venus*, 1810–30
Bronze, mercury gilding, marble, and glass
24 x 25 x 11 in. (62.3 x 64.8 x 28 cm) including glass dome
The New-York Historical Society, Bequest
of Goodhue Livingston, 1951 INV.235

Owned by the Livingston family of New York

24. French maker (Paris)
Covered compote, 1819–23
Silver
9 x 10 x 7 in. (23.5 x 25.4 x 19.8 cm)
Paris hallmarks on compote and cover
The New-York Historical Society, Bequest
of A. E. Gallatin, 1952.382ab

*Gift of the American Legation in Paris to Albert
Gallatin when he served as minister, 1816–23*

25. French maker (Paris)
Tea and coffee service, 1820–30
Porcelain, overglaze enamel decoration,
and gilding
Coffeepot: 10 x 7 x 4 in. (25.4 x 17.8 x 1 cm),
teapot: 7 x 7 x 4 in. (17.8 x 17.8 x 1 cm),
cream pitcher: 7 x 5 x 4 in. (17.8 x 12.8 x 1
cm), sugar bowl: 7 x 5 x 4 in. (17.8 x 12.8 x 1
cm), waste bowl: 4 x 8 in. (10 x 20.3 cm),
cups: 3 x 4 x 3 in. (7.5 x 10 x 7.5 cm),
saucers: 2 x 5 in. (5 x 12.8 cm)
The New-York Historical Society,
INV.12753ab–12773

*Owned by the Bayard/Rutgers families
of New York*

DOCUMENTS, PRINTS, AND BOOKS

26. Napoleon Bonaparte
    *Authorization to negotiate the sale of Louisiana
    to the United States*, 24 April 1803 (4 Floreal)
    Ink on vellum
    The New-York Historical Society,
    Gift of Mrs Goodhue Livingston, 1952

    *Signed by Napoleon Bonaparte, Robert R.
    Livingston, Charles Maurice de Talleyrand,
    François Barbé-Marbois, James Monroe, and
    Hugues-Bernard Maret*

27. Jean-Baptiste Wicar (French, 1762–1834)
    Joseph Bonaparte, 1807
    Engraving
    8¹/₁₆ in. (20.5 cm) diameter;
    paper 12⁷/₁₆ x 10¾ in. (31.5 x 27.2 cm)
    Inscribed: *Dessiné d'après nature par J.B.
    Wicar en 1807; Gravé par Guillaume Morghen.*
    Musée national du château de Malmaison,
    MM.4047.8265

28. Charles Percier (French, 1764–1838) and
    Pierre-François-Léonard Fontaine
    (French, 1762–1853)
    *Recueil de décorations intérieures comprenant
    tout ce qui a rapport à l'ameublement . . .*,
    Paris, s.n., 1801
    The Metropolitan Museum of Art, New
    York, The Thomas J. Watson Library
    (FIGURE 5)

    The Salle du Conseil at Malmaison, plate 55

29. Joseph Bonaparte, publisher
    (French, 1768–1844)
    Le Courrier des États-Unis, 1 March 1828
    The New-York Historical Society
    (FIGURE 8)

    *French-language newspaper published
    by Joseph Bonaparte in New York City
    beginning in 1828*

30. Pierre de la Mésangère (French, 1761–1831)
    Collection de meubles et objets de goût, vol. I,
    Paris, Au Bureau du Journal des dames,
    ca. 1801–31
    The New York Public Library,
    The Spencer Collection

    *Tabourets similar to those in the
    Salle du Conseil, plate 13*

31. Luigi Calamatta (Italian, 1802–1869)
    Still-Life with the Death Mask of Napoleon,
    1834
    Engraving
    18⁷/₈ x 14⁵/₈ in. (48 x 37 cm)
    Inscribed: *NAPOLEONE; Dessiné et gravé par
    Calamatta d'après le plâtre original moulé à
    Ste. Hélène / par le Docteur Antommarchi.*
    The New-York Historical Society

32. Anthony J. Bleecker
    (American, mid–19th century)
    *Catalogue of Rare, Original Paintings . . .
    Valuable Engravings, Elegant Sculpture,
    Household Furniture . . . Belonging to the
    Late Joseph Napoleon Bonaparte . . . to be
    sold . . . on Friday, June 25, 1847*
    The Metropolitan Museum of Art, New
    York, The Thomas J. Watson Library

33. J. D. Passavant, ed. (German, 1787–1861)
    *The Leuchtenberg Gallery: A Collection of
    Pictures Forming the Celebrated Gallery of his
    Imperial Highness the Duke of Leuchtenberg, at
    Munich.* Engraved by J. N. Muxel, Frankfurt,
    Joseph Baer, and London, G. Willis, 1852
    The Metropolitan Museum of Art, New
    York, The Thomas J. Watson Library
    (FIGURE 10)

    *Engraving of a fauteuil from the Salle du
    Conseil at Malmaison, plate 262*

34. Goullière (published by Furne, Paris)
    Josephine, mid–19th century
    Engraving
    8 x 5 in. (20.3 x 12.8 cm.)
    Inscribed: *Goullière sc.* and
    Publié par Furne, Paris
    The New-York Historical Society

35. Archibald Gracie King (on behalf of Louis
    Borg) to Andrew Warner, recording
    secretary of the New-York Historical
    Society, letter of 6 December 1867
    The New-York Historical Society

    *States Borg's intention to donate the Napoleon
    fauteuil to the New-York Historical Society*

36. Minutes of meeting of the New-York
    Historical Society, 20 December 1867,
    The New-York Historical Society

    Records Borg's gift of the Napoleon fauteuil

———— • ————

PHOTOGRAPHY CREDITS

FIGURES 1, 2, 9, 13, 18. Collection of the New-York Historical Society, New York (photographs by Glenn Castellano and Han Vu)

FIGURES 3–4, 11. Réunion des Musées Nationaux/Art Resource, New York

FIGURES 5, 10. The Thomas J. Watson Library, The Metropolitan Museum of Art, New York

FIGURE 6. Collection—Musée d'Art moderne et d'Art contemporain de la ville de Liège

FIGURE 7. Collection of the New Jersey Historical Society, Newark, Gift of Mrs. J. W. Mailliard (1957.62)

FIGURES 8, 17. Collection of the New-York Historical Society, New York (photographs by Glenn Castellano)

FIGURE 12. The Metropolitan Museum of Art, New York, Purchase, Joseph Pulitzer Bequest, 1943. (43.99) (photograph by Schecter Lee. Photograph © 1986 The Metropolitan Museum of Art)

FIGURE 14. The Historical Society of Pennsylvania (HSP), Philadelphia (3.1896)

FIGURE 15. Philadelphia Museum of Art, Philadelphia, Gift of Edward Hopkinson (1950-49-1)

FIGURE 16. Courtesy of Hirschl & Adler Galleries, New York

FIGURE 18

Jacob Frères, Armchair (*fauteuil*) from the Salle du Conseil at Malmaison, 1800 (CHECKLIST NO. 1)